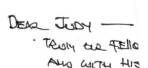

DEAR JUDY —
· TRULY OUR FELLO
AND WITH HIS

The Leadership of Jesus

15 OCTOBER 2000

Campbell McAlpine

Sovereign World

Sovereign World Ltd
PO Box 777
Tonbridge
Kent
TN11 OZS
England

ISBN 1 85240 281 4

This Sovereign World book is distributed in North America by Renew Books, a ministry of Gospel Light, Ventura, California, USA. For a free catalog of resources from Renew Books/Gospel Light, please contact your Christian supplier or call 1-800-4-GOSPEL.

Typeset by CRB Associates, Reepham, Norfolk.
Printed in England by Clays Ltd, St Ives plc.

Contents

Foreword

Many excellent books have been written on the subject of spiritual leadership, and we are indebted to all their authors. Also, in the Bible there are many role models from whom we can learn so much. The biographies of men like Moses, Joshua, David, Solomon, Peter, Paul and many others are honestly portrayed, recording both their successes and their failures. Our knowledge is enhanced not only by their spirituality but also their humanity. It is sometimes comforting to know that some of the 'greats' like the prophet Elijah were people *'with a nature like ours'*. As we read we admire their dedication, their seeking after God, their perseverance in adversity, but we also discover that some had times of depression, a sense of failure and many unanswered questions causing them to cry out, 'Why?'

Leaders can sometimes identify with the longing expressed by David,

> *'Oh, that I had wings like a dove!*
> *For then I would fly away and be at rest.*
> *Indeed, I would wander far off,*
> *And remain in the wilderness.'*   (Psalm 55:6–7)

Some not only felt that way but put feet to their desire, like Elijah who fled from the threats of a woman, Jezebel, only to be faced with the embarrassing question from the Almighty, *'What are you doing here, Elijah?'* (1 Kings 19:9). Or, how many leaders have had the same sentiments as Moses, who woke one morning, drew aside the tent door, only to discover they were still there! More than a million moaners and groaners, who the previous day had expressed their longing to be back in Egypt with its ample supply of garlic and cucumbers! He told God the greatest favour He could do for him was to kill him!

The subject of leadership is not merely confined to the realm of ministers, pastors and others who have a prominent role in the church or Christian organisations. A husband has a place of leadership, as does a mother as she influences her children (and her husband). The minimum requiring leadership is one. What wonderful work is done by Sunday school teachers, youth leaders, cell group leaders, and many others. The teaching in this book is applicable to many people. In everything the Lord Jesus is the perfect example. No one was ever born like Him. No one ever lived like Him. No one ever taught like Him. No one ever died like Him. No one ever rose like Him. No one ever **led** like Him. He is the incomparable Christ.

Jesus is the greatest leader who ever walked the earth. We are going to look at Him, listen to Him, learn from Him. He is the chief apostle, the greatest prophet, the most brilliant teacher, the most caring pastor, the most powerful evangelist. A small group of twelve submitted themselves to His leadership, having obeyed His call to follow Him. One of them, Judas, became a drop out. The rest in later years *'turned the world upside down'* (Acts 17:6). This was the fruit of the leadership of Jesus. May we too choose to follow Him and by His grace make an imprint on our generation for the Kingdom of God. The apostle Paul knew that one of the main purposes of his calling was *'to reveal His Son in me'* (Galatians 1:16). The more we learn of Him and from Him, the closer we walk with Him, the more we will be like Him, and the more He will be revealed in and through us. May the contents of this book promote a greater Christlikeness in both author and reader. The most important words in this book are the Scriptures. Read them carefully and prayerfully. The entrance of His word gives light.

I am so indebted to many Christian leaders who have blessed me and been examples, both those I have had personal contact with and also those who have taught me through their writings. I would like to list them, but it would be a long list, and I may inadvertently not mention some that I should. If by chance one of you is reading this, thank you. I am grateful. Also, how true are the words of Solomon: *'He who finds a wife finds a good thing, and obtains favour from the Lord'* (Proverbs 18:22). I am so thankful to God for Shelagh whose support in ministry for over fifty years has been so loyal. God gave her the privilege of founding an intercessory work among ladies called Lydia International Fellowship, now in so many nations. I am so thankful to these handmaidens of the Lord who have enriched my life with their prayers. And to all my family by whom I am so blessed for all the joy they give us. If we all got together there would be twenty-seven of us!

Of course all praise and thanksgiving goes to our precious Lord. This morning I was meditating in Psalm 123 and could not move far from the opening words, *'If it had not been the Lord who was on our side ... '.* Without Him the answer is always nothing. Blessed be the Lord.

Chapter 1

The Silent Years

Before anyone becomes a leader there is an unrecorded story of years of preparation and experience. Apart from one incident when Jesus was twelve years of age, we know nothing of His life from His birth, and the events immediately surrounding that wonderful time, until He was thirty years of age. That one event, which was so important, is an encouragement to those who work with young people. The family had been to Jerusalem and on the way home Mary and Joseph discovered that Jesus was missing (see Luke 2:41–50). Naturally perplexed they began to search for Him. 'Has anyone here seen Jesus?' It is always sad when Jesus is missing. After three days they found Him in the temple in Jerusalem, sitting with the teachers, listening to them and asking them questions. When Mary remonstrated with Him, He replied, *'Do you not know that I must be about My Father's business?'* At that age He had already decided that the most important thing in life was to serve God.

Jesus was brought up in a very devout family. He would have been well versed in the Torah, adhering to its instructions. He was the oldest in a family of brothers and sisters. Probably at about the age of fourteen, He began His apprenticeship as a carpenter under Joseph. He earned a living, was a member of the community and continued there until it was God's time for Him to leave this occupation to fulfil the ministry to which He was called. It would be wonderful to have a more intimate knowledge of these years, but Scripture is silent, leaving our curiosity unsatisfied. However, all these years were formative and an essential preparation for what lay ahead.

We also know little of the background of other biblical leaders. Apart from the story of his preservation as a baby we know so little about Moses, his upbringing in Egypt or his forty years prior to being called by God. What do we know of the preparation years of Abraham, Joshua, David, Solomon, Jeremiah, Ezekiel, John the Baptist or the twelve disciples? We know so little about the apostle Paul before his encounter with the living Christ on the Damascus road, apart from his persecution of the Church, and his own very brief mention of his religious upbringing. How important life is! We do not know the future, but God does. For every committed Christian God has a purpose, a plan, a preparation. When David Livingstone decided to be a doctor he did not know that God would use him to blaze a trail into the centre of Africa for the proclamation of the gospel of Jesus Christ, but God did. What are His plans for you? Some know His call; others do not, but are in a preparation time. As long as we say what Jesus said, *'I must be about my Father's business'*, then rest assured: He will lead, guide and make His purposes for your life clear. All that you are doing now is part of the divine programme, the formative years, the preparation time. How exciting!

It is interesting to note that Jesus was thirty years of age when He began His public ministry. By that age most people have reached maturity and decided the course of their life. David was thirty when he became king; Joseph was thirty when he became prime minister of Egypt; the Levites had to be thirty to fulfil their tasks in the tabernacle; Ezekiel was thirty when he began his prophetic ministry. Yes, it takes time and experience to prepare a leader. This of course does not mean that the Lord only uses leaders who are thirty years of age and over. Some years ago my wife Shelagh and I were ministering in a Church of Scotland in Dundee. Before leaving there on the Monday morning to go on to Edinburgh, I asked the minister with whom we were staying if we could stop at St Margaret's Church on the way to the station, to which he kindly agreed. In the front of the old church there is a cemetery in which is buried a previous minister, Robert Murray McCheyne, a Scottish Presbyterian. He was ordained at the age of twenty-three and died at the age of thirty. His godliness of life and powerful ministry left an imprint on Scotland that has never been forgotten. As we stood there we thanked God for his young servant, also asking Him to raise up leadership in Scotland of his calibre, commitment and consecration.

It has been my privilege over many years to teach and minister to many wonderful young men and women who are in God's preparation school, having resolved in their hearts to *'seek first the Kingdom of God and His righteousness'* (Matthew 6:33). The story of such preparation will probably never be written, but the fruit will be seen in future ministry and service. World events seem to be accelerating towards a climax. We are living in traumatic times and see the signs of the end times which Jesus indicated. Sometimes the question is asked, 'Where is the Church going?' The answer is, where she is led. The more like Jesus leaders are, the safer the Church is. He is our pattern, our example, our Lord and Master, the Head of the Church. What glory it is to know Him. What a privilege it is to serve Him. The great work of the Holy Spirit is to make us as much like Him as possible, so that the lasting impression of all we do is Jesus Himself.

I was once in a minister's office in a church in the USA and read a poem entitled *Indwelt*, by Beatrice Cleland, which he had framed on his desk. I am grateful for the simplicity of its sentiments.

Not merely in the words you say,
Not only in your deeds confessed,
But in the most unconscious way,
Is Christ through you expressed.

Is it just a beatific smile,
A holy light upon your brow?
O no. I felt His presence
When you laughed just now.

For me 'twas not the truth you taught,
To you so clear, to me so dim,
But when you came to see me,
You brought a sense of Him.

And from your eyes He beckons me,
And from your heart His love is shed,
Till I lose sight of you,
And see the Christ instead.

I am sure you with me would say 'Amen'.

Application

When God in His mercy saved us, He had a specific plan for our lives. He places us in His school, taking us from classroom to classroom. You may at present be in the period of the 'silent years', the time of preparation, or you may be fulfilling and developing your calling. It is interesting how He uses our skills, talents, professions for the fulfilling of His purposes. He chooses what we are and what we do for His Kingdom. For our part we must submit everything to His Lordship. Are we doing this? Every day is a further installment of our lives, seen by God as well as people. Take advantage of the **now** and see it as a precious opportunity of preparation and fulfilment of the divine plan for your life. Moses prayed, *'Teach us to number our days, that we may gain a heart of wisdom'* (Psalm 90:12). The popular poster says, '**Today** is the first day of the rest of your life'. One of the exciting things about being a Christian is we do not know how He is going to use us, or where He is going to take us. We do know that His will is good and perfect, as Paul stated:

'I beseech you therefore, brethren, by the mercies of God, that you present your bodies a living sacrifice, holy, acceptable to God, which is your reasonable service. And do not be conformed to this world, but be transformed by the renewing of your mind, that you may prove what is that good and acceptable will of God.'   (Romans 12:1–2)

Chapter 2

Into the Arena

When Jesus emerged from the 'silent years' there was no fanfare of trumpets, no heavenly choir as at His birth, no posters to announce His arrival, no public relations team to supervise His introduction. Matthew records the event with this simple statement: *'Then Jesus came from Galilee'* (Matthew 3:13). He joined a great crowd as they were listening to John the Baptist, who paused in his preaching, lifted his arm, pointed to Jesus, and declared, *'Behold! The Lamb of God who takes away the sin of the world'* (John 1:29). What an announcement! What an introduction! In a few days' time the Jews would be preparing the Passover feast. They would be selecting a lamb, shedding its blood and commemorating the mighty deliverance from the tyranny of Egypt which their ancestors had experienced. No doubt all eyes were turned to Him, the man called God's Lamb. The greatest leader of all time: God's Lamb. A lamb signified meekness and gentleness. His submissiveness was immediately demonstrated by His insisting that John should baptise Him, that He might *'fulfil all righteousness'* (Matthew 3:15). Within a short space of three-and-a-half years this Precious Lamb would be slain, His blood shed for the sins of the world.

Let's behold Him. We see in Jesus certain characteristics which are applicable to all leaders.

A Sense of Divine Vocation

Jesus knew, without any shadow of doubt that He was sent by God. There was a commission to be completed, a mission to be accomplished and a task to be fulfilled. Listen to the clarity of His heavenly calling:

> *'I know Him, for I am from Him, and He sent Me.'*
>
> (John 7:29)

> *'...I proceeded forth and came from God; nor have I come of Myself, but He sent Me.'*   (John 8:42)

Not only did He know that He had been sent, but He knew what He had been sent to do.

- **He came to serve**. Leadership is servanthood.

  > *'...the Son of Man did not come to be served, but to serve, and to give His life a ransom for many.'*
  >
  > (Matthew 20:28)

- **He came to preach.**

  > *'I must preach the kingdom of God to the other cities also, because for this purpose I have been sent.'*   (Luke 4:43)

- **He came to seek.**

  > *'For the Son of Man has come to seek and to save that which was lost.'*   (Matthew 18:11)

- **He came to be a light.**

  > *'I have come as a light into the world, that whoever believes in Me should not abide in darkness.'*
  >
  > (John 12:46)

- **He came to save the world.**

  > *'I did not come to judge the world but to save the world.'*
  >
  > (John 12:47)

- **He came to give life.**

  > *'I have come that they may have life, and that they may have it more abundantly.'*   (John 10:10)

- **He came to die.**

     'Now My soul is troubled, and what shall I say? "Father, save Me from this hour?" But for this purpose I came to this hour. Father, glorify Your name.'   (John 12:27–8)

- **He came to do the will of God.**

     'For I have come down from heaven, not to do My own will, but the will of Him who sent Me.'   (John 6:38)

Every true leader, called by God, will have that certain knowledge of their calling, and the assurance of God's enabling to fulfil it.

The Knowledge of Divine Anointing

The Lord Jesus knew that because God had called and sent Him, He had been given the anointing of the Holy Spirit to empower Him to do the work. At the start of His public ministry, in the synagogue in His home town of Nazareth, He opened the prophecy of Isaiah and read:

   'The Spirit of the Lord is upon Me,
   Because He has anointed Me to preach the
      gospel to the poor.
   He has sent Me to heal the brokenhearted,
   To preach deliverance to the captives
   And recovery of sight to the blind,
   To set at liberty those who are oppressed,
   To preach the acceptable year of the Lord.'

(Luke 4:18–19)

What a comfort to all leaders! God's call will always have God's anointing, that is His empowering by the Holy Spirit to fulfil the ministry. The term 'the Lord's anointed' was given to leaders chosen by God. God gave these instructions to Moses when Aaron and his sons were set apart for the priesthood:

> *'You shall anoint them, consecrate them, and sanctify them that they may minister to Me as priests ... And you shall take the anointing oil, pour it on his head and anoint him.'*
> (Exodus 28:41, 29:7)

I am sure there are few if any leaders who have not felt from time to time that they were not fit for their divine calling. Jeremiah's response to God's call was,

> *'Ah, Lord God. Behold, I cannot speak, for I am a youth.'*
> (Jeremiah 1:6)

When God called Gideon he said,

> *'O, my Lord, how can I save Israel? Indeed my clan is the weakest in Manasseh, and I am least in my father's house.'*
> (Judges 6:15)

Paul wrote to a timorous Timothy,

> *'God has not given us a spirit of fear, but of power and of love and of a sound mind. Therefore do not be ashamed of the testimony of our Lord, nor of me His prisoner.'*
> (2 Timothy 1:7–8)

Their sense of weakness was an essential qualification for their ministry. Paul said, *'when I am weak, then I am strong'* (2 Corinthians 12:10). Jesus said, *'I can of Myself do nothing'* (John 5:30). The prophet Zechariah declared,

> *' "Not by might nor by power, but by My Spirit,"*
> *Says the Lord of hosts.'* (Zechariah 4:6)

The Assurance of God's Choice

Every true leader has not only the sense of a divine calling, the assurance of God's anointing, but also the comfort of God's choosing. We cannot understand why He chose us, but the fact is He has, so we should embrace that choice with thanksgiving and wonder. Jesus was the Chosen One, as Peter declares:

'Coming to Him as to a Living Stone, rejected indeed by men, but chosen by God and precious.' (1 Peter 2:4)

At the cross the rulers sneered and mocked and said:

' "He saved others; let Him save Himself if He is the Christ, the chosen of God." ' (Luke 23:35)

Every true leader is a result of God's choice. Jesus chose the twelve disciples. Paul was a 'chosen vessel'. Many times God's choice would not be the human choice. Samuel was greatly impressed by the good-looking Eliab, a son of Jesse, but God told him that He did not look on the outward appearance but on the heart. David was God's choice to be King of Israel. How many times people have been voted in to leadership because of good appearance, business acumen, popularity, but have not been God's choice. The Risen Christ is the giver of ministries.

'He Himself gave some to be apostles, some prophets, some evangelists, and some pastors and teachers.'

(Ephesians 4:11)

What privilege, what grace to be chosen by Him! What a comfort the words of Jesus are:

'You did not choose Me, but I chose you and appointed you that you should go and bear fruit, and that your fruit should remain, that whatever you ask the Father in My Name He may give you.' (John 15:16)

What an honour to be a servant of the Most High God. It is an awesome calling. Sometimes I have borrowed the prayer of the late Dr A.W. Tozer, whose ministry and writings have been such a blessing to so many. Many will identify with the awareness of his need, his holy desires and his sense of

honour at being called by God, expressed in his prayer at his
ordination. After others had laid hands on him, and separ-
ated him to the work, he withdrew to be alone with God and
prayed:

'O Lord, I have heard Your voice and was afraid. You
have called me to an awesome task in a grave and
perilous hour. You are about to shake all nations and
the earth, and also heaven, that the things that cannot
be shaken may remain. O Lord, our Lord, You have
stooped to honour me to be Your servant. No man takes
this honour upon himself save he that is called of God,
as was Aaron. You have ordained me to be Your
messenger to them that are stubborn of heart and hard
of hearing. They have rejected You the Master, and it is
not expected that they will receive me, Your servant.
My God, I shall not waste time deploring my weakness
nor my unfittedness for the task. The responsibility is
not mine but Yours. You said, "I ordained you, I
sanctified you" and You have said also, "You shall go
to all that I send you, and whatever I command you,
you shall speak." Who am I to argue with You? or to
question Your sovereign choice. The decision is not
mine but Yours. So be it, Lord. Your will not mine be
done.

Well do I know, You God of the prophets and the
apostles, that as long as I honour You, You will honour
me. Help me therefore to make this solemn vow to
honour You in all my future life and labours, whether
by gain or loss, by life or death, and then keep that vow
unbroken while I live.

It is time for You to work, for the enemy has entered
Your pastures and the sheep are torn and scattered. False
shepherds abound who deny the danger, and laugh at
the perils that surround the flock. The sheep are
deceived by these hirelings and follow them with
touching loyalty, while the wolf closes in to kill and
destroy. I beseech You, give me eyes to detect the
presence of the enemy; give me understanding to

distinguish the false friend from the true. Give me vision to see and courage to report what I see faithfully. Make my voice so like Your voice that even the sick sheep will recognise it and follow You.

Lord Jesus, I come to You for spiritual preparation. Lay Your hand on me. Anoint me with the oil of a New Testament prophet. Forbid that I should become a religious scribe, and thus lose my prophetic calling. Save me from the curse that lies across the face of modern clergy; the curse of compromise, of imitation, of profes- sionalism. Save me from judging a church by its size, its popularity, or its yearly offering. Help me to remember that I am a prophet and not a promoter, not a religious manager but a prophet. Let me never become a slave to crowds. Heal my soul of earthly ambitions, and deliver me from the itch of publicity. Save me from the bondage to things. Let me not waste time puttering around the house. Lay Your terror on me, and drive me to the place of prayer where I may wrestle with princip- alities and powers, and the rulers of the darkness of the world. Deliver me from overeating or oversleeping. Teach me self-discipline that I may be a good soldier of Jesus Christ.

I accept hard work and small rewards in this life. I ask for no easy place. I shall try and be blind to the things that could make life easier. If others seek the smooth path, I shall try and take the hard without judging them too harshly. I shall expect opposition and try and take it quietly when it comes. Or, if, as sometimes it falleth to your servants, that I should have grateful gifts pressed upon me, stand by me then, and save me from the blight that so often follows. And if, in Your permissive will, honour should come to me from your church, let me not forget in that hour that I am unworthy of the least of Your mercies, and if men knew me as intimately as I know myself, they would withhold their honours and bestow them on others more worthy to receive them.

And now, O Lord of heaven and earth, I consecrate my remaining days to you. Let them be many or few, as You will. Let me stand before the great or minister to the poor and lowly, that choice is not mine, and I would not influence it if I could. I am Your servant to do Your will, and that will is sweeter to me than position or riches or fame, and I choose it above all things in heaven and earth. Though I am chosen by You and honoured by a high and heavenly calling, let me never forget that I am a man with all the natural faults and passions that plague the race of men. I pray You therefore, my Lord and my Redeemer, save me from myself, and from all the injuries that I may do myself while trying to be a blessing to others. Fill me with Your power by the Holy Spirit, and I will go in Your strength and tell of Your righteousness, even Yours only. I will spread abroad the story of redeeming love while my mortal powers endure.

Then, dear Lord, when I am old and weary and too tired to go on, have a place ready for me above, and make me to be numbered with Your saints in glory everlasting.'

Application

Thank God for Jesus, called, sent, chosen, anointed. Be encouraged. Still today, those whom He calls are chosen, sent, anointed. Those whom He sends He equips. Those whom He equips He uses. Those whom He uses He blesses. Blessed be the Name of the Lord.

Borrow the above prayer, and make it your own.

Chapter 3

The Perfect Example

In every aspect of His life Jesus was the perfect example for every leader. How wonderful that we have a written record of how He lived, how He taught, how He prayed, how He worked, how He responded to criticism, and how He led. He was the perfect example in everything. Peter reminds us that Christ suffered *'leaving us an example that* [we] *should follow His steps'* (1 Peter 2:21). John, too, exhorts us:

> *'He who says he abides in Him ought himself also to walk just as He walked.'*   (1 John 2:6)

Jesus showed us how to lead.

Leadership Is Serving Others

One day the disciples had a heated argument about which of them would be the greatest. To their embarrassment Jesus told them that He knew what they had been discussing, but instead of reprimanding them He gave them an example. Within a few hours Jesus would be betrayed, tried, condemned and crucified. They all met together in the upper room to commemorate the Passover. When the supper had ended, Jesus got up from the table, took off His outer garments, tied a towel round his waist, poured water into a basin, and knelt down and began to wash the disciples' feet. He fulfilled the servant's role. He knew that within a

few hours all of them would forsake Him. He knew Peter
would deny Him, Thomas would doubt Him, and Judas
would betray Him. When He had washed all their feet He
sat down again and said to them:

> *'Do you know what I have done to you? You call Me Teacher
> and Lord, and you say well, for so I am. If I then, your Lord
> and Teacher, have washed your feet, you also ought to wash
> one another's feet. For I have given you an example, that you
> should do as I have done to you.'*   (John 13:12–15)

Jesus had also told them:

> *' . . . whoever desires to become great among you, let him be
> your servant. And whoever desires to be first among you, let
> him be your slave – just as the Son of Man did not come to be
> served, but to serve, and to give His life a ransom for many.'*
>   (Matthew 20:26–8)

Yes, leadership is servanthood. It is not trying to attain to
position. Peter urged elders to **serve** as overseers, not to be
lords over those entrusted to them, and to be *'examples to the
flock'* (1 Peter 5:3). Jeremiah exhorted his hearers, *'do you seek
great things for yourself? Do not seek them'* (Jeremiah 45:5).
Jesus said, *'I do not seek My own glory'* (John 8:50). Someone
has said, 'If you want to know how much of a servant you
are, check your reactions when people treat you like one!'

Leadership Is Loving

When Jesus washed the disciples' feet He was not doing it out
of a sense of obligation, but out of a heart of sincere love.
That story is prefaced by the statement, *'having loved His own
that were in the world, He loved them to the end.'* He assured
them that the way people would be convinced that they were
His followers would be their obvious love for one another.
Love is Christlikeness. He gave them a clear instruction, not a
suggestion:

'A new commandment I give to you, that you love one another; as I have loved you, that you also love one another. By this all will know that you are My disciples, if you have love for one another.' (John 13:34–5)

The disciples had witnessed love in action all the time they had been with Him: love for the poor and oppressed; love for the lonely and misunderstood; love for the sick and sorrowing; love for the poor outcasts of society, and love for themselves. They had seen Him weep at the grave of Lazarus and heard the people say, *'See how He loved him!'* (John 11:36). They had seen Him weep over the city of Jerusalem. He was always the loving leader. Leadership without love does not profit. Paul clearly states to the Corinthians:

'Though I speak with the tongues of men and of angels, but have not love, I have become as sounding brass or a clanging cymbal. And though I have the gift of prophecy, and understand all mysteries and all knowledge, and though I have all faith, so that I could remove mountains but have not love, I am nothing.' (1 Corinthians 13:1–2)

How then can we be loving leaders? It is beyond the realm of merely liking people, or human affection. We cannot work it up, but God can work it out! Paul wrote that *'the love of God has been poured out in our hearts by the Holy Spirit who was given to us'* (Romans 5:5). We love with His love. The chorus says 'Jesus in me, loves you'. The fruit of the Spirit is love. Jesus was full of the Holy Spirit, so He was full of love.

Leadership Is Living

Leadership is living – that is, it is a demonstration of what we are. The Lord Jesus lived what He taught. He was the Word personified. He taught humility and was humble; He taught meekness and was meek; He taught mercy and was merciful; He taught purity and was pure; He taught love and was loving. He taught how to deal with persecution, misunderstanding, criticism and false accusation by always acting and reacting righteously. He taught the disciples how to pray, and He prayed. He taught truth and was truth. One day He challenged His accusers, *'Which of you convicts Me of sin?'* All they could do was bring false accusations. He is *'the way, the truth, and the life'* (John 14:6). Pilate was right when he said, *'I find no fault in this man'* (Luke 23:4).

The aim and desire of all leaders should be to **be** what we teach. Paul, writing to the Thessalonians, said:

> *'... you yourselves know how you ought to follow us, for we were not disorderly among you; nor did we eat anyone's bread free of charge, but worked with labour and toil night and day, that we might not be a burden to any of you, not because we do not have authority, but to make ourselves an **example** of how you should follow us.'*
>
> (2 Thessalonians 3:7–9)*

What a statement! What a challenge! How many leaders can sincerely say, 'Follow me'? Come into my home, see how I act and react, and follow me. See what I am like as a husband or wife, father or mother, and follow me. Listen to how I speak of others, and follow me. See how I handle my finances and follow me. See how I give and follow me. See how I pray and follow me. See what I watch and follow me. See how I hunger and thirst after God and follow me. Leaders demonstrate by doing. Francis of Assisi said, 'Preach Christ and if necessary use words.' Thank God that the same Holy Spirit who indwelt the Greatest Leader of all time is the same Holy Spirit who dwells in us. May He enable us to be more and more like Jesus. May people never have reason to say, 'I cannot hear what you are saying because of what you are.' The two on the road to Emmaus described Jesus as a *'Prophet mighty in deed and word before God and all the people'* (Luke 24:19). Paul exhorted the Colossians, *'whatever you do in word or deed, do all in the name of the Lord Jesus'* (Colossians 3:17). May God help us to match words with deeds, and deeds with words.

* Throughout the book all instances of emphasis in the Scriptures have been added by me.

Application

Praise the Lord for His perfect example. Ask Him to help us always to have a servant's heart, and not to seek great things for ourselves. Determine by His grace to be an instrument of His love, so that there will be ever-increasing evidence from His people that we belong to Him because of our love for each other. Are there things in our lives we would not approve of in the lives of those we lead? Are we good examples? Could we honestly say, 'Follow me'? All is available in Christ to make it so.

Chapter 4

Jesus the Praying Leader

For the disciples as they followed Jesus it was a very familiar sight to see Him lift His face towards heaven and speak to His Father. It seems that His usual practice was to pray with His eyes open. He was looking towards home. Nothing would distract Him from communion with God. He had taught His disciples that *'men always ought to pray and not lose heart'* (Luke 18:1), and He practised what He preached, thus demonstrating that all leaders should be praying leaders.

Jesus Prayed at all Times

* Early in the morning:

   'Now in the morning, having risen a long while before daylight, He went out and departed to a solitary place, and there He prayed.' (Mark 1:35)

* Late at night:

   'And when He had sent the multitudes away, He went up on a mountain by Himself to pray. And when evening had come, He was alone there.' (Matthew 14:23)

* All night:

   'Now it came to pass in those days that He went out to the mountain to pray, and continued all night in prayer to God.' (Luke 6:12)

Jesus Prayed Before Special Occasions

- At His baptism:

  'Now when all the people were baptized, it came to pass that Jesus also was baptized, and while He prayed, the heaven was opened.'   (Luke 3:21)

- Before choosing the twelve disciples:

  '. . . [He] continued all night in prayer to God. And when it was day, He called His disciples to Him; and from them He chose twelve whom He also named apostles.'

  (Luke 6:12–13)

- At His transfiguration:

  '. . . He took Peter, John, and James, and went up on the mountain to pray. And as He prayed, the appearance of His face was altered, and His robe became white and glistening.'   (Luke 9:28–9)

- In the garden:

  'He went away a second time and prayed, saying, "O My Father, if this cup cannot pass away from Me unless I drink it, Your will be done."'   (Matthew 26:42)

  'And being in an agony, He prayed more earnestly. And His sweat became like great drops of blood falling down to the ground.'   (Luke 22:44)

- On the cross:

  'Then Jesus said, "Father, forgive them for they do not know what they do."'   (Luke 23:34)

  'Father, into Your hands I commend My spirit.'

  (Luke 23:46)

Jesus Prayed for Different People

- For children:

  'Then little children were brought to Him that He might put His hands on them and pray, but the disciples rebuked them. But Jesus said, "Let the little children come to Me,

and do not forbid them, for of such is the kingdom of heaven."'
                                                    (Matthew 19:13–14)

- For His followers:

  'I pray for them. I do not pray for the world but for those whom You have given Me, for they are Yours.'

                                                    (John 17:9)

- For the discouraged:

  'Simon, Simon! Indeed, Satan has asked for you, that he may sift you as wheat. But I have prayed for you, that your faith should not fail; and when you have returned to Me, strengthen your brethren.'   (Luke 22:31–2)

- For His murderers:

  'Father, forgive them.'   (Luke 23:34)

- For the Church:

  'I do not pray for these alone, but also for those who will believe through their word.'   (John 17:20)

It was listening to Jesus praying that caused an unnamed disciple to say, 'Lord, teach us to pray, as John also taught his disciples' (Luke 11:1). We are indebted to the one who asked, and more indebted to the One Who responded. I trust that familiarity with this often repeated prayer will not cause it to lose its significance. There is no prayer like this one. It is so inclusive of all our needs and desires. It is a short prayer but every word is God breathed. I usually pray this prayer every morning when I awake, not I trust out of habit but out of a sense of great need as a new day begins. Imagine all Christians praying this prayer from the heart and meaning it! What unity would result? What relationships would be restored as all was forgiven? What sins would be avoided if we asked Him to deliver us from evil? What harmony would there be as we yielded our lives daily to obeying Him, and really meaning 'Your will be done'? What progress would there be in the world in His work if we really meant, and lived 'Your kingdom come'? What joy would be released if we all lived with the desire that in everything God would be glorified? O yes, Lord, teach us to pray.

Application

How is your prayer life? Do adjustments need to be made? When is the best time to make them? How wonderful it is to learn from Jesus. How gracious and forgiving He is, and what an encourager. He did not come into the world to condemn the world, or Christians, but to give life. Let us very thoughtfully, and slowly, and meaningfully pray:

'Our Father in heaven,
Hallowed be Your name.
Your kingdom come,
On earth as it is in heaven.
Give us this day our daily bread,
And forgive us our debts,
As we forgive our debtors.
And do not lead us into temptation,
But deliver us from the evil one.
For Yours is the kingdom and the power
*   and the glory forever.*
Amen.'   (Matthew 6:9–13)

Chapter 5

The Heart of Jesus

One day the Lord said to His disciples:

> 'A good man out of the good treasure of his heart brings forth
> good ... For out of the abundance of the heart his mouth
> speaks.'
> (Luke 6:45)

W.E. Vine describes the heart as 'the hidden spring of the personal life ... the seat of moral and spiritual life with its affections, perceptions, thoughts, understandings, including emotions, reason and will.' All this is so clearly revealed in all that Jesus said and did. We are given a wonderful insight into the heart of Jesus as a leader in His conversation with His Father and in His prayers for those He led. John 17 is sometimes referred to as the great intercessory prayer of the Lord Jesus. And so it is, but it is much more. It is Jesus giving an account to God of how He has led the men committed to Him, and His desires for them. There is so much to learn from what He said. From His words we learn the requirements of a leader, the work of a leader, and how a leader should pray for those in his or her care.

Let me remind you of the context. Within a few hours Jesus was going to die. He had been pouring out His heart to the disciples, knowing that He was going to leave them. He had already, as we have seen, demonstrated that every leader must be a servant by Himself taking the servant's place and washing their feet. He had commemorated the Passover with them and instituted what we call 'the Lord's supper' or communion. He told them plainly that He was going to return to heaven, where He would prepare a place for them, and that He didn't want their hearts to be troubled. He encouraged them by telling them that when He did leave them He would send 'another Comforter', the Holy Spirit who would be with them and in them, leading and guiding them and helping them to remember the words that He had spoken to them. He reminded them they would always be totally dependent on Him, and as long as they abided in Him and let His words abide in them, their lives would be fruitful and they would know the answers to their prayers. He told them honestly that following Him would not be easy. They would be hated and persecuted, and some would believe that by killing them they would be doing God a service. However, He told them to be of good cheer because He had overcome the world. Judas had been revealed as the traitor, and had left to do his dastardly work. Then, when Jesus had finished sharing with them, they left the upper room to make their way to the Garden of Gethsemane. Somewhere on the way they stopped, because Jesus had stopped, and they saw a familiar sight, Jesus lifting up His eyes to heaven.

Have you ever been in a house and walked into a room to discover someone on their knees praying? Almost instinctively you pause and tiptoe out, leaving the person to their devotions. We can almost feel this way as we read the intimate outpouring of Jesus' heart. We are on holy ground. A seventeenth-century preacher described this chapter in this way: 'it is the greatest prayer that was ever offered on earth, and it followed the greatest sermon that was ever preached on earth.' Let us not approach it as if we were merely reading another chapter in the Bible, but read it slowly, thoughtfully, meditatively with the prayer, 'Speak, Lord, for Your servant is listening.' These are some of the most important words in this book.

Jesus Prays for Himself
'Jesus spoke these words, lifted up His eyes to heaven, and said, "Father, the hour has come. Glorify Your Son, that Your Son also may glorify You, as You have given Him authority over all flesh, that He should give eternal life to as

*many as You have given Him. And this is eternal life, that
they may know You, the only true God, and Jesus Christ
whom You have sent. I have glorified You on the earth. I
have finished the work which You have given Me to do. And
now, O Father, glorify Me together with Yourself, with the
glory which I had with You before the world was."'*

Jesus Prays for His Disciples

*'"I have manifested Your name to the men whom You have
given Me out of the world. They were Yours, You gave them
to Me, and they have kept Your word. Now they have known
that all things which You have given Me are from You. For I
have given to them the words which You have given Me; and
they have received them, and have known surely that I came
forth from You; and they have believed that You sent Me. I
pray for them. I do not pray for the world but for those whom
You have given Me for they are Yours. And all Mine are
Yours, and Yours are Mine, and I am glorified in them.*

*Now I am no longer in the world, but these are in the
world, and I come to You, Holy Father, keep through Your
name those whom You have given Me, that they may be one
as We are. While I was with them in the world, I kept them
in Your name. Those whom You gave Me I have kept; and
none of them is lost except the son of perdition, that the
Scriptures might be fulfilled. But now I come to You, and
these things I speak in the world, that they may have My joy
fulfilled in themselves. I have given them Your word; and the
world has hated them because they are not of the world, just
as I am not of the world. I do not pray that You should take
them out of the world, but that You should keep them from
the evil one. They are not of the world, just as I am not of the
world. Sanctify them by Your truth. Your word is truth. As
You sent Me into the world, I also have sent them into the
world. And for their sakes I sanctify Myself, that they also
may be sanctified by the truth."'*

Jesus Prays for All Believers

*'"I do not pray for these alone, but also for those who will
believe in Me through their word; that they all may be one,*

as You, Father, are in Me, and I in You; that they also may be one in Us, that the world may believe that You sent Me. And the glory which You gave Me I have given them, that they may be one just as We are one. I in them, and You in Me; that they may be made perfect in one, and that the world may know that You have sent Me, and have loved them as You have loved Me. Father, I desire that they also whom You gave Me may be with Me where I am, that they may behold My glory which You have given Me; for You loved Me before the foundation of the world. O righteous Father! The world has not known You, but I have known You; and these have known that You sent Me. And I have declared to them Your name, and will declare it, that the love with which You loved Me may be in them, and I in them." '   (John 17)

Application

What can we say? What a Saviour! What an honour to be included in this wonderful prayer: *'I do not pray for these alone, but also for those who will believe... '*. Let us praise Him for saving us, calling us, desiring the very best for us, and showing us the way.

Chapter 6

The Requirements of a Leader
1: Intimate Fellowship with Father

The Lord Jesus was the most secure person who ever walked on the earth. One of the reasons for this was His intimate relationship with God, His Father. We have seen that as a boy of twelve He told Mary, *'I must be about My Father's business'*. Now, as He gives account of His leadership in John 17, He looks to heaven and says, *'Father'*. With all that lay ahead of Him He was secure in the knowledge that God loved Him:

> *'The **Father** loves the Son, and shows Him all things that He himself does; and He will show Him greater works than these, that you may marvel.'* (John 5:20)

He openly acknowledged His complete dependence on the Father for all that He did:

> *'Most assuredly, I say to you, the Son can do nothing of Himself, but what He sees the **Father** do; for whatever He does, the Son also does in like manner.'* (John 5:19)

His close communion with the Father is revealed in His continual communication with Him. We see this so clearly in the Gospels. At one time He sent out seventy of His followers to go in pairs to every place that He Himself would visit. When they returned they gave Him glowing reports of what had happened in their ministry. Jesus immediately looked up to heaven and said:

> *'I praise You, **Father**, Lord of heaven and earth, that You have hidden these things from the wise and prudent and revealed them to babes. Even so, **Father**, for so it seemed good in Your sight.'*   (Luke 10:21)

On another occasion, while walking with His disciples and sharing with them that He would soon die, He pauses and speaks to heaven, saying:

> *' "Now My soul is troubled, and what shall I say? '**Father**, save Me from this hour?' But for this purpose I came to this hour. **Father**, glorify Your name." Then a voice came from heaven saying, "I have both glorified it and will glorify it again." '*   (John 12:27–8)

Whether in joy or in sorrow there was always intimate fellowship. When Jesus stood at the grave of Lazarus, having told the onlookers to roll away the stone:

> *'[He] lifted up His eyes and said, "**Father**, I thank You that You have heard Me. And I know that you always hear Me, but because of the people who are standing by I said this, that they may believe that You sent Me." '*   (John 11:41–2)

Now, in this dramatic hour of prayer before being betrayed, bound, tried, condemned and crucified, there is still the same intimacy:

> *'**Father**, the hour has come.'*   (John 17:1)

> *'O **Father**, glorify Me together with Yourself, with the glory which I had with You before the world was.'*   (John 17:5)

> *'Holy **Father**, keep through Your name those whom You have given Me, that they may be one as We are.'*
>
> (John 17:11)

> *'**Father**, I desire that they also whom You gave Me be with
> Me where I am...'*   (John 17:24)

> *'O righteous **Father**, the world has not known You, but I
> have known You.'*   (John 17:25)

Father, Father, Father – such glorious closeness, trust, dependence, faith. When He came to the Garden of Gethsemane, He fell on His face and cried:

> *'O My **Father**, if it is possible, let this cup pass from Me,
> nevertheless, not as I will, but as You will.'*
> (Matthew 26:39)

and again:

> *'O My **Father**, if this cup cannot pass away unless I drink it,
> Your will be done.'*   (Matthew 26:42)

What an example! In spite of circumstances His confidence in His Father never wavered. Here was His strength, His comfort, His inspiration. He knew God. He always honoured God, therefore God always honoured Him. One day some Jews who claimed that God was their Father accused Him of having a demon. He told them:

> *'It is My Father who honours Me of whom you say that He is
> your God. Yet you have not known Him, but I know Him...'*
> (John 8:54–5)

'My Father... [and] *I know Him.'* Doesn't that stir something in your heart? God is my Father and I want to know Him. Daniel said:

> *'The people who know their God shall be strong, and carry
> out great exploits. And those of the people who understand
> shall instruct many...'*   (Daniel 11:32–3)

Just as relationship and fellowship with the Father was Jesus' strength, so it should be ours. Many Christians are very insecure, and therefore it is vitally important that leaders are secure themselves so that they can help others. What a glorious Father God is: Father of all creation; the Father of Israel by covenant; the Father of lights; the Father of glory; the Father of our Lord Jesus Christ, and by His grace the Father by adoption of every Christian.

'My Father ... Your Father'

Oh, the wonder of being brought into relationship with the Father through the death and resurrection of our blessed Lord Jesus.

> *'No one comes to the **Father** except through Me.'*
>
> (John 14:6)

> *' ... as many as received Him, to them He gave the right to become children of God, even to those who believe in His name ... '*   (John 1:12)

What a glorious message Jesus gave to Mary Magdalene on resurrection morning:

> *' ... go to My brethren and say to them, "I am ascending to My **Father**, and your **Father**, and to my God and your God.'*
>
> (John 20:17)

Every Christian can say 'my Father'. We can say to other Christians 'your Father'. Then we can all say together 'our Father'. We can all be secure in the knowledge of the Father's love:

> *' ... for the **Father** Himself loves you, because you have loved Me, and have believed that I came forth from God.'*
>
> (John 16:27)

Because He loves us, He delights to give to us:

> *' ... how much more will your **Father** who is in heaven give good things to those who ask Him?'*   (Matthew 7:11)

As a Father He gives His grace, mercy and peace. He also gives what Peter describes as *'exceedingly great and precious promises, that through these you may be partakers of the divine nature, having escaped the corruption that is in the world through lust'* (2 Peter 1:4). The more we know Him, the more effective we will be as leaders.

Application

How well do we know Father? How secure are we in Him? How often do we speak to Him, and address Him as Father, as Jesus did? Why not pause now and lift your eyes to heaven and say 'Father', as Jesus did.

Let's borrow Jesus' prayer:

*'**Father**, glorify Your name.'*

Note and imitate the reverence with which Jesus approached the Father:

*'Abba, **Father**, all things are possible for You.'*	(Mark 14:36)
*'**Father**, Lord of heaven and earth.'*	(Matthew 11:25)
'the only true God.'	(John 17:3)
*'O **Father**.'*	(John 17:5)
*'Holy **Father**.'*	(John 17:11)
*'O righteous **Father**!'*	(John 17:25)
*'Our **Father** in heaven, hallowed be Your name.'*	(Matthew 6:9)

Chapter 7

The Requirements of a Leader 2: Knowing God's Timing

Jesus said to the Father, *'the hour has come'* (John 17:1). He always knew the right time and the right timing. What an important lesson this is for us all. How often have we acted too slowly or too quickly, and how often have we missed the opportunity altogether? The Lord would be pushed neither by people, by circumstances nor even by needs. His desire was always to do the will of God both in action and timing.

When Jesus performed His first miracle at Cana of Galilee, He used the same expression but in the negative, *'My hour has not yet come.'* It was the embarrassing situation when the wine had run out at this special celebration. Mary came to Jesus and told Him, *'They have no wine.'* How many times previously had she wondered if this was the time and circumstance in which He would reveal who He really was? Perhaps she thought it would be when He was in His late teens, but no. Perhaps then in his early twenties? But again, no. The years pass one by one and now He is thirty! She may have given Jesus the information with a sense of expectancy. Jesus said to her, not unkindly:

> *'Woman, what does your concern have to do with Me? My hour has not yet come.'* (John 2:4)

What did Jesus mean? Simply that as yet God had not told Him to do anything about the situation. However, a little later, Father did show Him, and He turned the water into wine, but not when His mother tried to influence Him. All leaders are well aware that people often try to push them or influence them to take actions which are not always according to the will and timing of God. Jesus knew His absolute dependence on the Father. He said,

> *'Most assuredly, I say to you, the Son can do nothing of Himself, but what He sees the Father do; for whatever He does, the Son also does in like manner.'*   (John 5:19)

What a statement from the Son of God. *'I can do **nothing** of Myself.'* He only did **what** Father showed Him, and **when** He showed Him.

On another occasion His brothers tried to persuade Him to go up to Jerusalem to celebrate the Feast of Tabernacles. All the crowds would be there, and they urged Him,

> *'... go into Judea, that Your disciples also may see the works that You are doing. For no one does anything in secret while he himself seeks to be known openly.'*   (John 7:3–4)

They did not understand, neither at that time did they believe in Him. Here again He would not be pushed or influenced by His brothers, but said to them,

> *'My **time** has not yet come ... You go up to this feast. I am not yet going up to this feast, for My time has not yet fully come.'*   (John 7:6, 8)

He did go to Jerusalem – not when they wanted Him to but according to God's timetable.

Every leader should realise that there will be occasions when people will not understand their actions and timing. They will come with their questions, 'Why don't you ... ?' or 'When will you ... ?' Leaders must be prepared for this; God will vindicate obedience to His direction. It is easy to understand the misunderstanding and questions there must have been in Martha and Mary when Jesus did not immediately respond to the news that Lazarus was sick. Didn't He care? For two days He stayed in the place where He had received the news. His delay was not due to the fact that the last time He had been in Judea the Jews had tried to stone Him, or that He was not concerned for His friend Lazarus. The reason was simply that God had not told Him to go. God had greater purposes than a healing miracle, wonderful as that would be. Jesus made it clear to His disciples, who must also have been wondering why they hadn't left for Bethany where they had always received such wonderful hospitality, why He hadn't responded. He told them:

> *'This sickness is not unto death, but for the glory of God, that the Son of God may be glorified through it.'*
>
> (John 11:4)

As we will see later, the greatest desire in the heart of Jesus was that His Father God should be glorified, and the desire in the Father's heart was that His Son should be glorified. As a result of His obedience the disciples' faith in Him was going to be strengthened. He told them plainly, *'Lazarus is dead'* and then, no doubt to their utter amazement, He said,

> *'And I am glad for your sakes that I was not there, that you may believe. Nevertheless let us go to him.'*
>
> (John 11:15)

The time had come! There is a wonderful unhurriedness about the Lord Jesus. Never any panic. *'Whoever believes will not act hastily'* (Isaiah 28:16). Both Martha and Mary told Him later that if He had been there their brother would not have died. He said to Martha, *'Your brother shall rise again'*, and she replied that she knew about that, but it would be in the last day! Then He made that glorious statement:

> *'I am the resurrection and the life. He who believes in Me, though he may die, he shall live. And whoever lives and believes in Me shall never die. Do you believe this?'*
>
> (John 11:25–6)

Everything is 'on track' in God's programme. It is the right
day and the right hour. He comes to the grave, commands
the stone to be rolled away and, as they hesitate to obey,
encourages them:

> *'Did I not say to you that if you would believe you would see*
> *the glory of God?'*   (John 11:40)

The problem is now exposed, and still He does not hurry. He
lifts His eyes heavenward (*'The Son can do nothing of Himself'*)
and speaks to Father:

> *'Father, I thank You that You have heard Me. And I know*
> *that You always hear Me, but because of the people who are*
> *standing by I said this, that they may believe that You sent*
> *Me.'*   (John 11:41–2)

Then He cried with a loud voice – the voice that wakes the
dead:

> *' "Lazarus, come forth!" And he who had died came out . . . '*
>   (John 11:43–4)

As a result of His moving in God's way, at God's time, the
divine purpose was fulfilled. God was glorified; Jesus was
glorified, and His disciples believed in Him.

And now, in John 17, His hour had come. The greatest
hour in the world's history. Human beings are not in control
– God is. The power is not going to be in the hands of the
angry mob who would come with swords and clubs to take
Him prisoner. Neither would it be in the hands of those who
would crucify Him: *'No one takes* [My life] *from me, but I lay it*
down of Myself' (John 10:18). It is not a human agenda, it is
God's. Human beings have not chosen the timing of these
events: God has. The hour has come. The cross is God's plan.
It is the cross of our Lord Jesus Christ. What is happening is
what God had said would happen through the mouths of His
prophets. What the Jews had celebrated for centuries every
Passover Feast was about to be fulfilled, not in a lamb taken

from the flock, but in a Man, the Man Christ Jesus. The God Man. The Lamb of God who takes away the sin of the world. This is God's **timing:** the hour has come. He was born at the right time. He lived and worked at the right time. He died at the right time. He rose again at the right time. He ascended to heaven at the right time, and He is going to come again at the right time. As for God His way is perfect.

Solomon wrote:

'To everything there is a season.
A time for every purpose under heaven.
A time to be born
*   And a time to die.*
A time to plant
*   And a time to pluck what is planted.*
A time to kill,
*   And a time to heal.*
A time to break down,
*   And a time to build up.*
A time to weep
*   And a time to laugh.*
A time to mourn
*   And a time to dance.*
A time to cast away stones,
*   And a time to gather stones.*
A time to embrace,
*   And a time to refrain from embracing.*
A time to gain,
*   And a time to lose.*
A time to keep,
*   And a time to throw away.*
A time to tear,
*   And a time to sew.*
A time to keep silence,
*   And a time to speak.*
A time to love,
*   And a time to hate.*
A time of war,
*   And a time of peace.'*   (Ecclesiastes 3:1–8)

Let us desire the wisdom that the tribe of Issachar had, who *'had understanding of the **times**, to know what Israel ought to do'* (1 Chronicles 12:32).

Application

Let us thank the Lord Jesus for His wonderful example. Let us praise Him for doing everything at the right time, above all for dying for us, rising and ascending, and for the blessed hope that He is coming again – at the right time.

Let us ask His help to be led and moved by Him, and to be saved from doing anything as a result of being 'pushed' or being wrongly influenced: by people, circumstances or needs.

*'In **all** your ways acknowledge Him, and He shall direct your paths.'* (Proverbs 3:6)

'For as many as are led by the Sprit of God, these are the sons of God.' (Romans 8:14)

Chapter 8

The Requirements of a Leader 3: God-given Authority

> '...as You have given Him authority over all flesh, that He should give eternal life to as many as You have given Him.'
> (John 17:2)

In the leadership of Jesus we see that the person whom God calls is given divine authority. In the Greek the word translated 'authority' is *exousia*, which means the right, the privilege, the jurisdiction, the liberty to fulfil the task. Jesus had God's permission and approval to make it possible through His death and resurrection to give eternal life. Such God-given authority gives the confidence, encouragement and desire to complete what has been entrusted. Because His authority was God given people recognised it in what He did and said. They noticed the difference:

> 'And they were astonished at His teaching, for He taught them as one having authority, and not as the scribes.'
> (Mark 1:22)

This obvious authority angered the chief priests, elders, and scribes, who challenged Him:

> 'By what authority are You doing these things? And who gave You this authority to do these things?' (Mark 11:28)

In other words, where do you get what we do not have? Jesus didn't give them a direct answer, but asked them where they thought John the Baptist had received his authority: from heaven or from men? His question put them on the spot. If they said it was from God, they knew that Jesus would challenge them with the question, 'Why didn't you believe him?' If, on the other hand, they said the authority was man-originated, they would be in big trouble because most of the people believed that John had been a true prophet sent by God. So they squirmed out of the situation by saying, 'We do not know.' Jesus told them if they would not honestly answer a straight question, He would not answer their question.

One of the obvious reasons why Jesus had this authority was not only because it was God given, but also because He continually lived under the authority of the Father. His great desire was not to do His own will, but the will of God. If we desire to have authority, we must be **under** authority. This is so clearly illustrated in the well-known story of the healing of the centurion's servant. When the centurion heard that Jesus was in the area he sent men to Him, pleading for Him to come and heal his servant. As Jesus was approaching the house, however, he sent some friends to meet Him with this message:

> *'Lord, do not trouble Yourself, for I am not worthy that You should enter under my roof. Therefore I did not even think myself worthy to come to You. But say the word, and my servant will be healed. For I am also a man placed under authority, having soldiers under me. And I say to one, "Go," and he goes; and to another "Come," and he comes; and to my servant, "Do this," and he does it.'* (Luke 7:7–8)

Jesus marvelled at the centurion's statement and told the people, *'I have not found such great faith, not even in Israel!'* Whatever the centurion ordered was immediately obeyed, but this was because he himself immediately obeyed what he was told. The lesson is so clear. We cannot have authority unless we are under authority. Jesus said to His Father, *'not what I will, but what You will'* (Mark 14:36). What a comfort to all leaders. God will always give us His authority – the right, privilege, permission to do whatever He commissions us to do – as long as we obey Him.

Authority and Power

The Lord Jesus had not only the authority, *exousia*, but also the power, *dunamis*. Authority is wonderful, but without the power – that is, the ability to see the task to completion – it is useless. One day as Jesus was teaching in the synagogue in Capernaum He was interrupted by the cries of a demon-possessed man. When He cast out the evil spirit, the amazed congregation said:

> *'What a word this is! For with authority and power He commands the unclean spirits, and they come out.'*
>
> (Luke 4:36)

Jesus was filled with the power of the Holy Spirit. At the beginning of His public ministry, the Holy Spirit came upon Him, and Luke tells us that *'Jesus being filled with the Holy Spirit, returned from the Jordan and was led by the Spirit into the wilderness . . . '* (Luke 4:1). After forty days He *'returned in the power of the Spirit'* (Luke 4:14). He went to Nazareth and in the synagogue read Isaiah's prophecy:

> *'The Spirit of the Lord is upon Me,*
> *Because He has anointed Me to preach*
> * the gospel to the poor.*
> *He has sent Me to heal the brokenhearted,*
> *To preach deliverance to the captives*
> *And recovery of sight to the blind;*
> *To set at liberty those who are oppressed,*
> *To preach the acceptable year of the Lord.'*
>
> (Luke 4:18–19)

Having read the Scriptures, He closed the book, and with all eyes fixed on Him, said:

> *'Today this scripture is fulfilled in your hearing.'*
>
> (Luke 4:21)

After the Lord Jesus had died and risen from the dead, and just before returning to heaven, He gave His disciples authority to take the gospel to the world:

> *'All authority has been given to Me in heaven and on earth. Go, therefore, and make disciples of all the nations, baptizing them in the name of the Father and of the Son and of the Holy Spirit, teaching them to observe all things that I have commanded you; and lo, I am with you always, even to the end of the age.'*   (Matthew 28:18–20)

Wonderful though it was to be given such authority from the One who has all authority, it was not sufficient for their momentous task. They needed more than authority: they needed power. Therefore He instructed them:

> *'Behold, I send the promise of My Father upon you; but tarry in the city of Jerusalem until you are endued with power from on high.'*   (Luke 24:49)

> *'...He commanded them not to depart from Jerusalem, but to wait for the Promise of the Father, "which," He said, "you have heard from Me, for John truly baptized with water, but you shall be baptized with the Holy Spirit not many days from now ... you shall receive power when the Holy Spirit has come upon you; and you shall be witnesses to Me in Jerusalem, and in all Judea and Samaria, and to the end of the earth."'*   (Acts 1:4–5, 8).

They obeyed His word, believed His promise, and on the day of Pentecost:

> *'...suddenly there came a sound from heaven, as of a rushing mighty wind, and it filled the whole house where they were sitting. Then there appeared to them divided tongues as of fire, and one sat upon each of them. And*

they were filled with the Holy Spirit and began to speak with other tongues, as the Spirit gave them utterance.'

(Acts 2:2–4)

Now they had authority and power, and they went and turned the world upside down! Thank God, the same power is available to all and to every leader. Paul exhorted the Ephesians to be *'filled with the Spirit'* (Ephesians 5:18). Not only do we need to be filled, but we also need to go on being continually filled with the Spirit. We need to be filled to have power. We need to be filled so that the fruit of the Spirit becomes evident in our lives. We need to be filled so that the gifts of the Spirit become real in our lives: the word of wisdom, the word of knowledge, faith, healings, miracles, prophecy, discerning of spirits, tongues and interpretation of tongues (see 1 Corinthians 12:1, 7–10).

Among the readers of this book there may be those who know that God has called them to serve Him, that He has given them the authority to serve Him, and yet are conscious of powerlessness and may be asking, 'How can I have the power of the Holy Spirit to enable me to fulfil my calling?' There is only one Person to whom we can go for the answer: the Lord Jesus. Remember the words He spoke on the great day of the feast:

'If anyone thirsts, let him come to Me and drink. He who believes in Me, as the Scripture has said, out of his heart will flow rivers of water. But this He spoke concerning the Spirit, whom those believing in Him would receive; for the Holy Spirit was not yet given, because Jesus was not yet glorified.'
(John 7:37–9)

Jesus said, *'If anyone thirsts . . . '* The first requirement is a sense of need. What is it to be thirsty? It is to feel dry and know it! The next requirement is a clean heart. The Holy Spirit can never fill any area of our life where there is sin. Sin needs to be acknowledged, confessed and repented of, before receiving His forgiveness on the basis of promise:

> *'If we confess our sins, He is faithful and just to forgive us*
> *our sins and to cleanse us from all unrighteousness.'*
>
> (1 John 1:9)

With our thirsty and cleansed hearts we accept His invitation, *'come to Me and drink.'* What is it to drink? When you are thirsty you drink a glass of water; by doing so you are receiving it. Drinking is receiving. Then Jesus said, *'Believe'*. Ask, receive, believe. That is how we were saved. We had a sense of our need because of our sins, and we came to Jesus with these needs. He invited us to receive Him and to believe His promise on the basis of knowing that He died for our sins and rose from the dead. When we did this we were saved, and the Holy Spirit gave us the witness that we were sons of God. In the same way we come to Him to be filled with the Holy Spirit. Ask, receive, believe. In most instances in the Acts of the Apostles when people were baptised in the Spirit for the first time, they spoke in new languages. Using their tongues, the Holy Spirit spoke to God in a language they did not know. On the day of Pentecost when the disciples spoke in tongues, some of the people present spoke those very languages and were able to understand that they were speaking about the *'wonderful works of God'*. How wonderful that the Holy Spirit can use our tongues to praise and glorify God, unlimited by our human restrictions! However, the purpose of being filled with the Holy Spirit is not to receive tongues but to receive power.

Given to Give

The Lord Jesus acknowledged that God had given Him authority so that He could give it to others, *'... as You have given Him authority..., that He should give...'* (John 17:2). Our desire to receive from the Lord should never be for self-exaltation, self-promotion, or self-satisfaction, but rather that we may be better equipped to bless others. Jesus once said to His disciples, *'Freely you have received, freely give'* (Matthew 10:8). He also said, *'It is more blessed to give than to receive'* (Acts 20:35). Jeremiah the prophet asked the question, '... *do you seek great things for yourself? Do not seek them'* (Jeremiah 45:5). The great work of the Holy Spirit is always to glorify the Lord Jesus.

Application

Let us thank the Lord Jesus for being the perfect example of serving the Father with authority and power.

Let us be filled with the Spirit. If you have never experienced this, why not come to the Lord Jesus now. Come with a cleansed heart; deal with everything which is not of God. Come to Him: ask, receive, believe.

Let us be sure that we are not seeking great things for ourselves, but desire only to glorify God and exalt the Lord Jesus.

Chapter 9

The Requirements of a Leader 4: Clarity of Purpose

'...that they may know You, the only true God, and Jesus Christ whom You have sent.'   (John 17:3)

What a privilege to continue to look and listen to the Lord Jesus. The Pharisees wanted to arrest Jesus but the officers they sent returned empty-handed. When they were asked, *'Why have you not brought Him?'* they replied, *'No man ever spoke like this Man'* (John 7:46). How true. No one ever spoke like Him. He told His disciples one day, *'The words that I speak to you are spirit, and they are life'* (John 6:63).

What clarity of purpose Jesus had. And we should have the same, that people might know God and His Son Jesus Christ. Jesus' primary purpose was not to bring us to Himself, but to bring us to God. The problem was that the human race had lost relationship with their Creator. Sin had caused separation, and we were powerless to remedy the situation. No one human being was able to help anybody else because everyone was in the same condition: *'all have sinned and come short of the glory of God'* (Romans 3:23). What a disastrous plight! The situation was hopeless: human beings were faced with eternal death. But the answer to eternal death is eternal life and, thank God, that was why Jesus came.

'I came that they may have life, and that they may have it more abundantly.'   (John 10:10)

He had such a clear purpose. Let us with thankful hearts remind ourselves of the great reasons for His coming:

- **To bring us to God:**

  *'Christ also suffered for sins, the just for the unjust, that He might **bring us to God**.'* (1 Peter 3:18)

  *'I am the way, the truth, and the life. No man **comes to the Father** except through Me.'* (John 14:6)

- **To make us children of God:**

  *'But as many as received Him, to them He gave the right to become **the children of God**, even to those who believe in His name.'* (John 1:12)

- **To reconcile us to God:**

  *'For if when we were enemies we were **reconciled to God** though the death of His Son, much more, having been **reconciled**, we shall be saved by His life.'*

  (Romans 5:10)

- **To hear His purpose, His longing, and make it ours:**

  *'. . . that they may **know You**, the only true God, and Jesus Christ whom You have sent.'* (John 17:3)

Strength Comes through the Knowledge of God

As leaders we have to be convinced that knowing God and making Him known are our top priorities. There is no greater knowledge on earth than the knowledge of God. If we agree with this it will be demonstrated in our own pursuit of the knowledge of Him. **Who** we know is more important that **what** we do. Activities should never supercede this holy quest. Paul exhorted the Ephesians to *'be **strong** in the Lord and in the power of His might'* (Ephesians 6:10). Churches may boast of their numerical strength, or their many activities, their missionary vision or their traditions, but Jeremiah gives this salutary counsel:

> ' "Let not the wise man glory in his wisdom,
> Let not the mighty man glory in his might,
> Nor let not the rich man glory in his riches;
> But let him who glories glory in this,
> That he understands and knows Me,
> That I am the Lord, exercising
>   lovingkindness, judgment, and
>   righteousness in the earth.
> For in these things I delight," says the Lord.'
>
> (Jeremiah 9:23–4)

If we ever want to make a spiritual assessment, either personally or corporately, we can ask ourselves a very simple question, 'How well do I/we know God?' Daniel said, *'the people who know God shall be strong'*. Over a hundred years ago a young 21-year-old minister opened his morning sermon with this statement:

> 'It has been said by someone that the proper study of mankind is man. I will not oppose the idea, but I believe it is equally true that the proper study of God's elect is God. The proper study of a Christian is the Godhead. The highest science, the loftiest speculation, the mightiest philosophy, which can ever engage the attention of a child of God, is the name, the nature, the person, the work, the doings, and the existence of the Great God whom he calls his Father. There is something exceedingly improving to the mind in a contemplation of the Divinity. It is a subject so vast, that all our thoughts are lost in its immensity; so deep, that our pride is drowned in its infinity. No subject of contemplation will tend more to humble the mind than thoughts of God.'

The young minister was Charles Haddon Spurgeon, whose life and ministry blessed so many throughout his life. The privilege and responsibility of those to whom God has given the task of caring for His people, is to *'feed the church of God, which He hath purchased with His own blood'* (Acts 20:28, AV).

Someone has said, 'God has sent me to feed the sheep, not to amuse the goats.'

Every leader who has made an impact in their realm of responsibility, is marked out by a common trait: they are people who know God. But, more than this, they have a continual consciousness of their great need to know Him more. Hear the cry of Moses, who probably knew God better than anyone else in his day, *'show me Your way, that I may* **know** *You'* (Exodus 33:13) or the longing of David,

> *'As the deer pants for the water brooks,*
> *So pants my soul for You, O God.*
> *My soul thirsts for God, for the living God.*
> *When shall I come and appear before God?'*
>
> (Psalm 42:1–2)

Or the cry of Paul, *'that I may* **know Him** *and the power of His resurrection, and the fellowship of His sufferings, being conformed to His death'* (Philippians 3:10). The effectiveness of leaders is in equal proportion to their knowledge of God.

What a debt of gratitude we owe to the Lord Jesus for showing us what God is like: *'He who has seen Me has seen the Father'* (John 14:9). He is the *'express image of His person'* (Hebrews 1:3). He showed the heart of God, the love of God, the compassion of God, the power of God, the righteousness of God, the holiness of God, the character of God. He was *'God manifested in the flesh'* (1 Timothy 3:16). Paul encouraged the Ephesians to be *'followers of God'* (Ephesians 5:1) or, as the Amplified Bible puts it, *'imitators of God'*. We can only imitate what or who we know. Let us use every means available to increase in our knowledge of Him. Our main source of course is the Word of God, and our main teacher the Holy Spirit, who, Jesus promised, would lead us into all truth. What a desperate need there is today for a renewed love for God, demonstrated by a renewed love for His Word, with hearts that will obey. How much the Church needs shepherds to feed the flock, teachers to unfold the wonders of God, and all of us to learn of and from Him.

Application

Let us embrace the purpose of Jesus *'that they may know You, the only true God, and Jesus Christ whom You have sent.'*

What about our personal desire to know God? Have we lost our thirst? Have we changed our priority? Are there adjustments that need to be made?

Have our activities crowded out our fellowship with Him?

He is always a very present help in time of need. Sometimes we only have to pray a very short prayer, 'Help me.'

Chapter 10

The Requirements of a Leader 5: Purity of Motive (i)

'I have glorified You on the earth.'   (John 17:4)

Having had a glimpse into the purpose of the leadership of Jesus, we are now going to consider His motive. One of the many truths Jesus taught us is that **why** we do something is just as important as **what** we do. He rebuked the Pharisees for wanting their righteous deeds to be seen by people to receive their approval, and reminded them that while men and women look on the outward, God looks on the heart. People are impressed by activity, but God is impressed by obedience. It was said of certain Old Testament kings that they *'did what was good and right in the sight of the Lord'* (see, for example, 2 Chronicles 14:2). Everything that is good is not necessarily right in the sight of God. It is good to pray, but not right in the sight of the Lord to pray with an unforgiving heart. It is good to fast, but not right in the sight of the Lord to fast to be seen by people. It is good to give to the poor, but again not right in the sight of the Lord to give in order to be noticed. It is good to take communion, but not right to do so without examining our hearts and without discerning the Lord's Body.

'I Have Glorified You on the Earth'

In these few words Jesus expressed to His Father the reason behind everything He did, *'I have glorified You . . . '*. To glorify means to honour, to magnify, to praise, to put first. His great desire was that in everything He did God should get all the credit and all the praise. The purity of this intent charac- terised His total life from Bethlehem to Calvary. On the first Christmas morning the silence of the night was shattered by a multitude of heavenly beings, praising God and saying:

> *'**Glory to God** in the highest and on earth peace, good will toward men.'*   (Luke 2:14)

As at His birth so at His death. When He cried with a loud voice on the cross, *'Father, into Your hands I commit My spirit'* and breathed His last, the centurion who was overseeing the crucifixion and had witnessed all that had happened, *'**glori- fied God**, saying, "Certainly this was a righteous Man!"'* (Luke 23:47). Not once is it ever recorded in the Gospels that anyone ever came to Jesus and said, 'You are such a wonder- ful Person.' This is remarkable. He was wonderful. He is wonderful. *'His name shall be called Wonderful'*, but every- thing He did brought glory to God. When He healed the paralysed man, we read:

> *'Now when the multitudes saw it, they marveled and **glorified God**, who had given such power to men.'*
> (Matthew 9:8)

One day He healed a whole multitude, and it is recorded:

> *'So the multitude marveled when they saw the mute speak- ing, the maimed made whole, the lame walking, and the blind seeing, and they **glorified the God** of Israel.'*
> (Matthew 15:31)

When He walked into the village of Nain, and saw a widow on her way to bury her son, He brought him back to life, and

> *'Then fear came upon all, and they **glorified God**, saying, "A great prophet has risen among us"; and "God has visited His people."'*   (Luke 7:16)

When Jesus loosed a woman from a spirit of infirmity which had bound her for eighteen years, we read:

> *'And He laid His hands on her, and immediately she was made straight, and **glorified God**.'*   (Luke 13:13)

When a blind man from Jericho cried out to Jesus to have mercy on him, He responded,

> *'And immediately he received His sight and followed Him, **glorifying God**. And all the people, when they saw it, gave **praise to God**.'*   (Luke 18:43)

When Jesus received word that Lazarus was sick, He said:

> *'This sickness is not unto death, but for the **glory of God**, that the Son of God may be glorified through it.'*
>
> (John 11:4)

How true were the words of Jesus: *'I have glorified You on the earth.'* Let's face it. There is something in all of us which wants some of the credit for what we do. How many have been offended because they felt unappreciated and have not been thanked for what they have done? How many times have we been depressed and disappointed because no one has recognised our talents and abilities? The servant is not greater than his master. They rejected Him, they did not appreciate Him, they crucified Him. Do you still want to be a leader? Whose glory are we seeking?

Paul gives us a wonderful insight into the heart of Jesus. He had made a decision:

> *'[He] made Himself of no reputation, taking the form of a servant, and coming in the likeness of men. And being found in appearance as a man, He humbled Himself and became obedient to the point of death, even the death of the cross.'*
>
> (Philippians 2:7–8)

Jesus was a 'no reputation' leader. Many leaders want to build a good reputation; they want to be well respected and well spoken of or written about. May we never be more concerned about what people think of us than what God thinks of us. Well can I remember God in His grace and mercy dealing with me on this point once while I was involved in a national outreach. One morning, while I was meditating on this verse about Jesus being of no reputation, the Holy Spirit in His great faithfulness convicted me of sin. I wanted God to have almost all the glory in the work, but after all Campbell McAlpine was involved. I saw the awfulness of wanting any credit for what God could do. He showed me the shame of wanting credit. He broke me, and I wept and repented, confessing the pride of my heart. He asked me to go to the cross and totally surrender any desire for any glory. I yielded to Him any desire to be 'well known' and cried to Him to give me the ability by the Holy Spirit to do all for His glory. There was such a release. No longer did I ever need to impress anyone – my reputation was no longer at stake. Everything within me cried, 'To God be the glory.' No reputation. Nothing to defend.

Remember the story of Moses when he was on Mount Sinai spending time with God (see Exodus 32). God told him that the people had turned to idolatry and were worshipping a golden calf. He said He was ready to destroy the people, and make a new great nation from Moses's descendants. Moses refused the offer, being more concerned about what the Egyptians would say about God – that He could bring them out of Egypt, but could not bring them into the Promised Land. As far as Moses was concerned it was God's glory that was at stake, not his own personal reputation or advancement.

When Jesus said these words to the Father, *'I have glorified You on the earth'*, the cross was only a few hours away. His purpose for coming into the world was going to be accomplished. He was going to be put to so much shame, but in it all He was going to honour God and make a way for countless millions in future years to fulfil the purpose for which they were created. The catechism states, 'Man's chief end is to **glorify God** and to enjoy Him forever.'

Application

What is your motive as a spiritual leader? Do you seek great things for yourself? Why not be like Jesus, and be willing to be a no reputation person? Go by faith to the cross and there lay down every desire to build anything for yourself.

Let us determine that by His grace our motive will always be to glorify God and exalt the Lord Jesus. If the motive is right, the work will be right.

Chapter 11

The Requirements of a Leader
5: Purity of Motive (ii)

'Do All to the Glory of God...'

In the previous chapter we saw that behind every activity of
the Lord Jesus, there was purity of motive. He wanted to
glorify the Father. As this is of such vital importance in the
life of every leader, and every Christian, let us see how it can
be applied to our lives.

When Paul wrote to the church at Corinth, he knew that
many of the members of the church there had been saved out
of a life of extreme idolatry. It was a common practice at
many banquets in the city to offer some of the food to idols
before eating. The apostle foresaw a difficult situation which
might face a Christian attending one of these feasts. Before
starting to eat his food another Christian might approach
him and tell him that the food had been offered to idols.
What should he do? Paul wrote that for the sake of the
conscience of the person who gave the information, he
should not eat it. Then he added:

> *'Therefore, whether you eat or drink, or whatever you do,* ***do
> all to the glory of God.'***   (1 Corinthians 10:31)

Do **all** to the glory of God. That includes every aspect of
living: our home, our marriage, our business, our friendships,
our sports activities, our church. This kind of living is neither

legalistic nor restrictive, but rather liberating and enjoyable, for the will of God is the safest and happiest situation in which anyone can live. This is how Jesus lived, and He was the most fulfilled Person who ever walked the earth.

Sometimes we are faced with decisions and are uncertain what we should do. When there is doubt it is good to ask the question, 'Which decision would glorify God, honour Him, put Him first, cause others to acknowledge Him?' Something may appear both pleasurable and attractive, but if it will not glorify God, it will be harmful and unfruitful. We should be convinced always that God's will is perfect, and therefore acceptable to us. This obviously raises a question as to whether there is anything in my life which does not glorify Him? Is there a habit, relationship or activity, which is contrary to the will of God? What does the Word say? *'Do all to the glory of God.'*

Praise Glorifies God

The Word of God is extremely practical, showing not only what we should do, but how we can do it. We can learn so much from David who had such a capacity to worship, praise and extol God. The Psalms proclaim God's majesty, glory, righteousness, wonder and sovereign power. One of the greatest things about worshipping God is that God is glorified. David wrote:

> *'Whoever offers praise glorifies Me;*
> *And to him that orders his conduct aright*
> *I will show the salvation of God.'* (Psalm 50:23)

How wonderful. Every time we worship the Lord, praise Him and thank Him, we glorify Him. What an encouragement to praise Him more, not only in church but when we're at home, out walking, or travelling in the car. Wherever we are, we can thank Him for His goodness, for who He is, for the wonders of His creation, for health, strength, family and friends, and so much more. We can daily praise Him that our names are recorded in heaven. We can bless Him for all His goodness and mercy, for His love and provision. No wonder the closing words in the Psalms are,

> *'Let everything that has breath praise the Lord.'*
>
> (Psalm 150:6)

Faith Glorifies God

How else can we glorify Him? Paul reminded the Romans that Abraham was a man who trusted God, gaining for himself the name 'faithful Abraham'. As a result of this confidence in the Almighty God:

> *'He did not waver at the promise of God through unbelief, but was strengthened in faith, **giving glory to God**, and being fully convinced that what He had promised He was also able to perform.'*   (Romans 4:20–2)

What an incentive to believe and trust God! God is glorified. Abraham simply believed that God was God, that whatever God said was true, and that whatever He promised He would fulfil. When we trust Him, we are proclaiming who He is – the faithful God. What an encouragement also to get to know Him better. The more we know Him, then the more we trust Him.

Just as faith glorifies God, then it is obvious that unbelief and doubt dishonour Him. Remember the story of Zacharias? He was engaged in his duties in the temple when suddenly an angel appeared to him with the message that his prayers had been heard, and that he and his wife Elizabeth would have a son whom they were to call John (see Luke 1:5–25). For many years they had prayed for a child but nothing had happened, and now they were both old. When Gabriel gave him this astonishing announcement Zacharias did not believe. The angel told him that because of his unbelief he would be struck dumb. So for nine months he could not verbally share with Elizabeth the anticipated joy of the longing of their hearts. When the baby was born all the relatives and friends gathered together to celebrate at the naming ceremony. Most thought that the little boy would be named after his silent dad. However Elizabeth was adamant that he should be called John, the name given to them by Gabriel. While the people were remonstrating they turned to Zacharias and asked him to write down what the name should be. He wrote, *'His name is John'* (Luke 1:63). As soon as he confessed what the angel had instructed, his mouth was opened, he was filled with the Holy Spirit and **glorified God**.

The faith that glorifies God is not just some great faith to do some great deed, but the day-to-day commitment of our lives, works and ways to Him, trusting and relying on Him to lead us, keep us, supply our every need and enable us to do His will.

Bearing Fruit Glorifies God

How glorious it is to know that every Christian has the life of Christ living in them. His life is a holy life, a pure life, a powerful life, a fruit-bearing life. Jesus taught His disciples:

> *'I am the vine, you are the branches. He who abides in Me, and I in him, bears much fruit, for without Me you can do nothing.'*   (John 15:5)

Fruitfulness is the evidence of a right relationship with Jesus Christ and fellowship with Him. The fruit that is produced in our lives is love, joy, peace, long-suffering, gentleness, goodness, faith, meekness and self-control. His life is also revealed in and through us in being a blessing to others. However, the greatest thing about fruit bearing is that **God is glorified**. Jesus said:

> *'By this My Father is **glorified**, that you bear much fruit; so you will be My disciples.'*   (John 15:8)

Answered Prayer Glorifies God

Every prayer of Jesus was answered because He never asked the Father for anything that would not glorify God. In talking with the disciples He had encouraged them with these words:

> *'And whatever you ask in My name, that I will do, that the* **Father may be glorified** *in the Son. If you ask anything in My name, I will do it.'*   (John 14:13–14)

What prayers are answered? The prayers that have the desire to glorify God. When Jesus had taught His disciples to pray, He concluded with these words, *'For Yours is the kingdom and the power, and* **the glory** *forever. Amen.'*

Good Works Glorify God

When Jesus was teaching the disciples in what is known as the 'Sermon on the Mount' He encouraged them to live as those who were in a new kingdom, the Kingdom of God. He included this instruction:

> *'Let your light so shine before men, that they may see your good works, and* **glorify your Father** *in heaven.'*
>
>   (Matthew 5:16)

He emphasised that the motive behind being good, and doing good works, should be to glorify God. Later Jesus would rebuke the Pharisees and the scribes for doing good works to gain the approval of people: *'But all their works they do to be seen by men'* (Matthew 23:5). They wanted human approval more than God's approval, and that would be the only praise they would ever receive. In contrast Jesus taught His disciples:

> *'Take heed that you do not do your charitable deeds before men to be seen by them. Otherwise you have no reward from your Father in heaven. Therefore, when you do a charitable deed, do not sound a trumpet before you as the hypocrites do in the synagogues and in the streets, that they may have glory from men. Assuredly, I say to you, they have their reward. But when you do a charitable deed, do not let your*

left hand know what your right hand is doing, that your charitable deed may be in secret; and your Father who sees in secret will Himself reward you openly.'   (Matthew 6:1–4)

There is no greater approval than God's approval. When our motive is to glorify Him, He promises a heavenly recompense.

' . . . seek first the kingdom of God and His righteousness, and all these things shall be added to you.'   (Matthew 6:33)

God Should Be Glorified in Our Bodies and Spirits

Paul reminded the church at Corinth:

*' . . . do you not know that your body is the temple of the Holy Spirit who is in you, whom you have from God, and you are not your own? For you were bought at a price, therefore, **glorify God in your body and in your spirit**, which are God's.'*   (1 Corinthians 6:19–20)

What a truth! The Spirit of God lives in us. Our bodies are likened to a temple, a church, a holy place where God lives. They have been purchased at a great price so that God may be honoured in and through them. If this were truly understood and applied, there would be less adultery, fornication and uncleanness in the Church of the living God.

I was once preaching in a church in Copenhagen, Denmark. At the end of the service a young lady came to me and, without any preliminary remarks, said, 'I do not see anything wrong with smoking.' I hadn't mentioned smoking in the message; I had been speaking about fire, not smoke! I asked her why she was telling me, and she said that she just wanted me to know! She told me she was a Christian, and I asked her why she hadn't smoked in church. She assured me she would never do that, so I asked her why. She said, 'Because it is the church of God.' I told her that was most interesting, as the Bible describes our bodies as the temple of the Holy Spirit, so if she wouldn't blow smoke in the church, why blow it into her body which is His temple?

Paul also spoke about our spirits, making it clear that we should be careful how we feed our spirits. I once heard a story about the cuckoo. Ornithologists tell us that the cuckoo, which is found in Europe and is so named because of the sound it makes, is a very lazy bird, and if possible will avoid building a nest, often laying its eggs in the nests of other birds. In the story a cuckoo, flying around looking for somewhere to deposit her eggs, spied and took advantage of a thrush's nest which had just one egg in it. Soon afterwards mother thrush returned, and although she was sure there was only one egg when she left home, and the second one was larger than the first, with all her maternal instincts she sat on both eggs till they were hatched. One day, having gone to get food for the offspring, she returns to find two open mouths clamoring to be fed. The truth is that the one she feeds is the one that is going to grow! We still have two natures, the old and the new, and the fact is that the one we feed is the one that is going to grow.

> *'For those who live according to the flesh set their minds on the things of the flesh, but those who live according to the Spirit, the things of the Spirit. For to be carnally minded is death, but to be spiritually minded is life and peace.'*
>
> (Romans 8:5–6)

Unity Glorifies God

David's words are so well known:

> *'Behold how good and how pleasant it is*
> *For brethren to dwell together in unity.'*   (Psalm 133:1)

as are the words of Jesus to His disciples:

> *'By this shall all men know that you are My disciples if you love one another.'*   (John 13:35)

Unity not only makes life much more pleasant and makes the atmosphere much friendlier, but, most importantly of all, true unity **glorifies God**, while disunity dishonours Him. How significant Paul's words are:

> *'Now may the God of patience and comfort grant you to be like-minded toward one another, according to Christ Jesus, that you may with one mind and one mouth **glorify the God and Father** of our Lord Jesus Christ.'*
>
> (Romans 15:5–6)

Let us pray for, practise, and work for unity. May we be instruments of unity so that His name will be honoured, and people might see we are what we claim to be.

Glorifying God in Death

After Jesus had risen from the dead, He met some of His disciples at the sea of Tiberias. They had been fishing all night but had caught nothing. They saw a man standing on the shore who shouted to them to cast their nets on the right side of the boat, and, when they did so, they netted a huge catch. When they brought their boat to the land they recognised that the man, who had breakfast ready for them, was Jesus. Later on that morning Jesus asked Peter three times if he loved Him, and then told Peter something of how he was going to die when he was an old man. If the historians are correct Peter was crucified upside down after watching as his wife was martyred. Those who witnessed this must have been horrified at such an end to a life which had been lived for Jesus. However, John, referring to what Jesus said, wrote,

> *'This He spake, signifying by what death he would **glorify God.'***
>
> (John 21:19)

A life lived; a work finished; a death died: *'Whatever you do, do **all to the glory of God**.'*

How Can We Live to the Glory of God?

Jesus gives us the perfect pattern. Everything He did had the right motive: *'I have **glorified** You on the earth.'* God would never ask us to live this way without making it possible. Remember Jesus told His disciples that after He had gone He would send the Holy Spirit, who would **glorify** Him. The very same Spirit in Jesus who enabled Him to glorify God would be the same Holy Spirit in them – and in us. What is the evidence of the Spirit-filled life? That life **glorifies God** and exalts the Lord Jesus.

Application

To live to glorify God is initially a choice. Jesus said, *'I do not seek My own glory'* (John 8:50) so let's choose, or confirm the choice we have already made.

Let us ask God to help us, by the Holy Spirit, to glorify Him by praising Him, trusting Him, bearing fruit, praying according to His will, glorifying Him in our bodies and spirits, being instruments of unity, doing good works, and living and dying for His glory.

Chapter 12

The Requirements of a Leader 6: The Goal of a Leader

'I have finished the work You have given Me to do.'
(John 17:4)

As we have looked at the leadership of the Lord Jesus we have seen the importance of having the right purpose and also the right motive. We also see He had the right goal, the right aspiration, the right intention. That aim was to finish, to complete, His God-given mission that *'the world through Him might be saved'* (John 3:17). How gloriously He accomplished it. The cry came from the cross, *'It is finished!'*

For the Lord Jesus doing the work of God was not merely completing an assignment but it was a joy:

'...who for the joy that was set before Him endured the cross, despising the shame, and has sat down at the right hand of the throne of God.' (Hebrews 12:2)

Leaders need to demonstrate that serving God is a real joy, a delight. One of the accusations brought against the children of Israel was:

'...you did not serve the Lord with joy and gladness of heart, for the abundance of all things.'
(Deuteronomy 28:47)

Let us embrace that Christlike desire to complete the work delegated to us. The Lord Jesus never tried to get followers under false pretences. He encouraged them to count the cost, not only considering the beginning but also the end. He made it clear that to be His disciple meant putting God first in everything: before human relationships, before personal ambition and before any desire for material possessions. Speaking of a person who was about to build a tower He suggested that the right thing to do before starting was to sit down and count the cost, in order to calculate whether he had enough resources to be able to finish it. He pointed out the folly of laying foundations and then being unable to complete the building, thus becoming a laughing stock. Jesus knew that the finishing of His task would mean rejection, suffering and death, but He never wavered. He fulfilled all the conditions for finishing.

Determine, Begin, Finish

Solomon undertook the great task committed to him by God of building the temple. His life illustrates some of the steps involved in completing a goal.

Solomon determined to build

> *'Solomon determined to build a temple for the name of the Lord.'*   (2 Chronicles 2:1)

God had told David, Solomon's father, that his son would build the temple. It was His will and His timing. Solomon never wanted it to be known as 'Solomon's temple'. He wanted to build a temple for the name of the Lord and for His Kingdom and, knowing it was God's will, he **determined** to do it. Life is punctuated by our choices and determinations. Jesus determined. He chose to do the will of God. In spite of all that lay before Him, *'His face was set for the journey to Jerusalem'* (Luke 9:53). Daniel *'purposed in his heart that he would not defile himself with the portion of the king's delicacies'*

(Daniel 1:8). When Paul went to the church at Corinth with all its problems, he said,

> *'I determined not to know anything among you except Jesus Christ and Him crucified.'*   (1 Corinthians 2:2)

Moses determined: *'choosing rather to suffer affliction with the people of God than to enjoy the passing pleasures of sin'* (Hebrews 11:25). When God calls people to follow Him a choice has to be made, a determination established.

Solomon began to build

It is great to determine, but better to determine and **begin**. Some have heard the call of God to some ministry, service or country. That is wonderful – but it is useless unless we begin. It is written of Jesus, He *'began to preach'* (Matthew 4:17).

It is interesting to notice where Solomon began to build the temple: *'on Mount Moriah, where the Lord had appeared to his father David at the place that David had prepared on the threshing floor of Ornan the Jebusite'* (2 Chronicles 3:1). David had made the mistake of taking a census of Israel. Having been rebuked by the prophet Gad for his reliance on people instead of God, which resulted in 70,000 men dying, he was told to go and erect an altar to the Lord. He came to this piece of ground owned by Ornan. Ornan offered to give it to him for nothing, but he said, *'I will surely buy it for the full price'* (1 Chronicles 21:24). So the place where Solomon began to build was the place of the full price. That is the place for all of us to begin: the place of the full price. We are not our own. Jesus Christ is Lord. Jesus said,

> *'... whoever of you does not forsake all that he has cannot be My disciple.'*   (Luke 14:33)

Solomon finished

It is right to determine, and better to determine and begin, but better still to determine, begin and **finish**. Jesus determined. Jesus began. Jesus finished. Between the beginning and the finishing there are a great variety of experiences and continual choices. There are sometimes temptations to give up and turn back. There are times of difficulty and disappointment, times of frustration and fear, times of approval and times of antagonism. None of you who are reading this have finished yet. Remember your determination: no turning back. In Luke 9:57–62 we read about some people's responses to following Jesus. One man came to Jesus and said, *'I will follow you wherever You go.'* Jesus told him that, if he did follow Him, there would be times when he like Him would have no place to lay his head. Jesus called another man who said that he would follow Jesus after his father had died. Another person said he would follow Jesus, but first he wanted to have a farewell party with his friends. Jesus told him:

> *'No one, having put his hand to the plough, and looking back, is fit for the kingdom of God.'* 		(Luke 9:62)

Solomon determined, began and **finished**. In this way God was glorified, and the temple was filled with the glory of God. As we have already seen this is the purpose of all that we do, that in everything God will be glorified.

I am sure all of us would want to say at the end of our lives: 'I have glorified You on the earth. I have finished the work You gave me to do.' Thank God we can look *'unto Jesus, the author and the **finisher** of our faith'* (Hebrews 12:2), again knowing that the same Holy Spirit who enabled Him to finish, can also enable us. We can say with Paul: *'being confident of this very thing, that He who has begun a good work in you will **complete** it till the day of Jesus Christ'* (Philippians 1:6). Let us lift our eyes to the future, to eternity, and to the finishing line. One great preacher used to cry, 'I want to live for eternity. I want to preach for eternity. I want to work for eternity. I want only God.'

I do not agree with the statement, 'Don't be too heavenly minded or you will be no earthly use.' The more heavenly minded we are, the more earthly use we are. Jesus was always heavenly minded. The hymnwriter encourages us:

Turn your eyes upon Jesus,
Look full in His wonderful face,
And the things of earth will grow strangely dim,
In the light of His glory and grace.

Amen.

The Finishers

Our perfect example is Jesus. Let us take a brief look at some other people who finished well.

David

What a life and what a love for God he had! He had trials and testings; he sinned grievously and was forgiven generously; he was a shepherd, a soldier, the sweet psalmist of Israel, a husband, father and friend, and the King of Israel. He was a man after God's heart, who did God's will. How did he finish?

> *'David, after he had **served his generation**, by the will of God fell asleep, and was buried with his fathers...'*
>
> (Acts 13:36)

Paul

What an amazing farewell speech Paul writes from his prison cell as he awaits his executioner. What a life! What a ministry! What hardships and what victories!

> *'I have fought the good fight, I have **finished** the race, I have kept the faith. Finally there is laid up for me the crown of righteousness, which the Lord, the righteous Judge, will give to me on that Day, and not to me only, but also to all who have loved His appearing.'*   (2 Timothy 4:7–8)

One day I was driving with a friend in London when he stopped his car outside a cemetery and told me he wanted to show me a grave. On the tombstone were written these words: 'I have fought a good fight, I have finished the course,

I have kept the faith.' It was the burial place of Charles Haddon Spurgeon, often described as 'the prince of preachers'. We stood there and prayed, thanking God for this special servant of His, and putting in a postscript for ourselves: 'Lord, please help us to finish well.' In the same cemetery I was attracted to a large memorial where I read the inscription: 'To the memory of Baron Rothschild who died with the satisfaction of knowing that he had left behind the richest stocked bank in Europe.' We were both convinced that Charles Spurgeon had done the right thing by laying up treasure in heaven where neither rust nor moth can corrupt nor thieves break in and steal. All that could be said of the Baron was 'he left behind' every centime.

Peter

He was another great finisher, who also continued his ministry from prison writing to others and encouraging and exhorting them:

> *'Therefore, brethren, be even more diligent to make your calling and election sure, for if you do these things you will never stumble; for so an entrance will be supplied to you abundantly into the everlasting kingdom of our Lord and Saviour Jesus Christ. Therefore I will not be negligent to remind you always of these things, though you know them, and are established in this present truth. Yes, I think it right, as long as I am in this body to stir you up by reminding you, knowing that shortly I must put off my tent, just as our Lord Jesus Christ showed me.'* (2 Peter 1:10–14)

He could also say, 'I have finished the work.' What a wonderful way to describe death, *'put off my tent'*. He was about to go from the temporal into the eternal.

Stephen

Stephen was a deacon in the early Church, who openly preached the truth in spite of opposition and became the first martyr in the new Church era. How did he finish?

'... he, being full of the Holy Spirit, gazed into heaven and saw the glory of God, and Jesus standing at the right hand of God ... And they stoned Stephen as he was calling on God, and saying, "Lord Jesus, receive my spirit." Then he knelt down and cried out with a loud voice, "Lord, do not charge them with this sin." And when he had said this, he fell asleep.' (Acts 7:55, 59, 60)

He finished praying, as Jesus had done – triumphant.

And there are so many more, *'of whom the world was not worthy.'*

Non-finishers

King Saul

He started well, determined, began. God appointed him as commander over his inheritance and gave him *'another heart'* (1 Samuel 10:9). The Spirit of God came on him, and he prophesied. Samuel declared before the people that the Lord had chosen him. However, he failed to finish. He allowed envy, bitterness and hatred against David to enter his heart. His own sad confession was, *'I have played the fool and erred exceedingly'* (1 Samuel 26:21). We see the possibilities of what might have been, the tragedy of what was.

Judas

He also started well, determined, began. As one of the twelve whom Jesus called apostles he preached the gospel of the Kingdom, healed the sick and for three-and-a-half years followed Jesus. He listened to the greatest teaching anyone ever heard, but he didn't finish. He allowed the enemy to come in and influence his life. He pilfered the petty cash. He sold Jesus for thirty pieces of silver. Jesus said of him: *'It would have been good for that man if he had never been born'* (Mark 14:21). What a disappointment.

Sadly there are many others: King Uzziah: a wonderful king who made a good start and a bad finish; Solomon with all his great wisdom and writings, and yet sadly at the end: *'his wives turned his heart after other gods; and his heart was not loyal to the Lord his God, as was the heart of his father David'* (1 Kings 11:4); Demas was a man close to Paul and yet he wrote these sad words: *'Demas has forsaken me, having loved this present world and has departed'* (2 Timothy 4:10). However God is the God of great grace and mercy, who restores the fallen when they repent and acknowledge their need. They may be like a Jacob and have a limp for the rest of their lives, but like him, when he came to the end of his journey, they also can be a blessing. We read,

> *'By faith Jacob, when he was dying, blessed each of the sons of Joseph and worshipped, leaning on the top of his staff.'*
> (Hebrews 11:21)

A great finish, blessing others and worshipping God.

How Will We Finish?

In order to give an accurate assessment of that question we have to ask ourselves: How am I doing **now**? Am I doing the will of God **now**? Am I fulfilling the ministry God has given me **now**? Or has something come in between the beginning of the work and the finishing line? Remember:

> *'The gifts and the calling of God are irrevocable.'*
> (Romans 11:29)

If we have stopped, let's start again. Jesus took back a denying Peter and a doubting Thomas. He restored a repentant David. His blood is sufficient to cleanse, His Spirit sufficient to empower, His grace sufficient to keep. His Word is sufficient to teach, and the world is there to reach.

Application

Determine, begin, finish.

> *'Now to Him who is able to keep you from stumbling,*
> *And to present you faultless*
> *Before the presence of His glory with exceeding joy,*
> *To God our Saviour,*
> *Who alone is wise,*
> *Be glory and majesty,*
> *Dominion and power,*
> *Both now and forever. Amen.'*   (Jude 23–5)

Chapter 13

The Requirements of a Leader 7: Stewardship

'...those whom You have given Me...'　　　　(John 17:9)

The Lord Jesus knew that the men He led had been committed to Him by God, His Father. Six times in John 17 He refers to them as those given to Him. Sixty-five times in this comparatively short chapter He refers to them in other ways (i.e. 'the men', 'they', 'them', 'those', 'these', 'their'). What a requisite this is for all leaders, whether caring for few or many. How good it is for a pastor of a church, a Sunday school teacher, a young people's leader, a group leader, etc., to look at the people and say, 'those whom You have given to me'. True, some would not have been their choice. Who would have chosen Judas Iscariot? When the apostle Paul was giving his farewell message to the elders of the church at Ephesus, he exhorted them:

> *'Therefore take heed to yourselves and to all the flock, among which the Holy Spirit has made you overseers, to shepherd the church of God, which He has purchased with His own blood.'*　　　　(Acts 20:28)

Paul reminds them of the value God puts on those whom they lead: *'purchased with His own blood'*. Peter also, in his first epistle, reminds leaders that they are shepherds, not of a denomination or a group, but of the 'flock of God'. Just as Jesus is now giving an account to the Father of how He cared for the disciples, so every leader will one day have to give an account of how they fulfilled their leadership. Peter wrote:

> *'Shepherd the flock of God which is among you, serving as overseers, not by constraint but willingly, not for dishonest gain but eagerly, nor as being lords over those entrusted to you, but being examples to the flock; and when the Chief Shepherd appears, you will receive the crown of glory that does not fade away.'*   (1 Peter 5:2–4)

What a privilege to care for *'His flock'*! What a responsibility *'entrusted to you'*! What a reward: *'a crown of glory that does not fade away.'* What authority you have been given: *'the Holy Spirit has made you . . . '*. I remember reading a story of a minister of a church who came down to breakfast looking ghastly pale. When his wife asked him if he was all right he told her he had had a terrible dream in the night. In the dream he was standing before God who asked him, 'Where are the souls of the people I gave to you?' and he could only reply, 'I don't know.' 'Where are the souls of the young people, and the people I sent to your house?' Again he had to reply, 'I don't know.' His wife said, 'Don't worry, dear,' and he dropped dead. This is certainly a dramatic story, but God still speaks through dreams. Thank God for all leaders who love and care for those entrusted to them.

Parents

What privilege and responsibility God gives to parents too! How important it is that leaders have a good record in their own homes and families. Paul included this as a qualification for leaders:

> *' . . . one who rules his own house well, having his children in submission with all reverence (for if a man does not know how to rule his own house, how can he take care of the church of God?).'*   (1 Timothy 3:4–5)

This is a fair question. Jacob described his offspring as *'the children whom God has graciously given your servant'* (Genesis 33:5). How can we be good stewards of God's family if we are not good stewards of our own? Many of us have so much to be grateful for in being brought up in homes where God was honoured, and parents loved us and sought to nurture us in the knowledge of our Lord Jesus. Some have not had that privilege but can start a new generation of followers of Jesus. How much leaders need God's wisdom and direction not to neglect their families while seeking to help others. Eli, the priest, was a leader who failed to discipline his own sons with the result that they later came under the judgement of God. David was a bad example to his family in the matter of Bathsheba and, although God in His grace forgave him, there were repercussions in his own children. Let us seek God's grace, help and wisdom to be good stewards of our own families, and God's.

The Requirements of Good Stewards

Holiness of life

When Paul wrote to Titus he gave him a list of requirements for spiritual leaders. He had been given the task of appointing leaders in the new churches and had this 'checklist':

> *'... blameless, the husband of one wife, having faithful children not accused of dissipation or insubordination. For a bishop must be blameless as a steward of God, not self-willed, not quick-tempered, not given to wine, nor violent, nor greedy for money, but hospitable, a lover of what is good, sober-minded, just, holy, self-controlled, holding fast the faithful word as he has been taught, that he may be able, by sound doctrine, both to exhort and convict those who contradict.'*   (Titus 1:6–9)

Faithfulness

Jesus once asked the question, *'Who then is that faithful and wise steward?'* (Luke 12:42). He answered by saying that the faithful steward was a man diligently carrying out all his duties because he expected his master to return at any time. Paul wrote:

> '... *it is required in stewards that one be found faithful.*'
> (1 Corinthians 4:2)

To be faithful is to be trustworthy, reliable, dependable, day by day carrying out the duties God has given us to fulfil. I like the expression the Puritans used: 'the perseverance of the saints'. Faithfulness is going on for God in spite of everything and everybody, completely dependent on Him. How holy Jesus was; how faithful Jesus was and is.

Wisdom

The second part of Jesus' question quoted above concerned the 'wise steward'. Wisdom is insight, the ability to discern and to apply to our lives and circumstances the word and the will of God. We all know how insufficient mere human wisdom is to do the work of God. Jesus was wisdom personified. Everything He did was absolutely right. He didn't make mistakes, or wrong judgements, or wrong statements. One day when he was teaching in the synagogue in his home town of Nazareth, the people asked the question, *'Where did this Man get this wisdom and these mighty works?'* (Matthew 13:54). He got it from the same source that is available to us. How very kind of God to offer us all the wisdom we need. I love the promise given through James. I take it every morning because every morning I am a candidate.

> *'If any of you lacks wisdom, let him ask of God, who gives to all liberally and without reproach, and it will be given to him. But let him ask in faith, with no doubting.'*
> (James 1:5–6)

A leader will never have to face any situation without having God's wisdom available. And what wonderful wisdom it is!

> *'...the wisdom that is from above is first pure, then peace-*
> *able, gentle, willing to yield, full of mercy and good fruits,*
> *without partiality and without hypocrisy.'*   (James 3:17)

It has been my practice for many years to read a chapter of Proverbs each day. The key word in this book is wisdom. It is not about the wisdom of Solomon, but the wisdom that God gave to Solomon. His wisdom is a guide to charter our course in life, to save us from mistakes, to help us make the right decisions. The acquiring of wisdom is through the word of God. Read these words thoughtfully and prayerfully as they are essential for all good stewards:

> *'My son, if you **receive** my words,*
> *And **treasure** my commands within you,*
> *So that you **incline** your ear to wisdom,*
> *And **apply** your heart to understanding.*
> *Yes, if you **cry** out for discernment,*
> *And lift up your voice for understanding.*
> *If you **seek** for her as silver*
> *And **search** for her as for hidden treasures;*
> ***Then** you will understand the fear of the Lord*
> *And find the knowledge of God.*
> *For the **Lord gives wisdom;***
> *From His mouth come knowledge and understanding.'*
>
> (Proverbs 2:1–6)

Application

Let us praise the Lord for His perfect stewardship.

Let us ask God for His help to be good stewards in our own households. Are there any adjustments to be made?

Let us thank God for those He has given us to steward. Remember one day we have to give Him an account, and the Lord wants to give us a crown of glory.

Let us pursue holiness, faithfulness and wisdom. Take the promise for those who ask for wisdom and by faith receive it. Make it a morning by morning request. Don't leave home without it!

Chapter 14

The Work of a Leader

'I must work the works of Him who sent Me while it is day;
the night is coming when no one can work.'   (John 9:4)

We have been looking at the Lord Jesus and learning from
Him the requirements of spiritual leadership. We have seen:

- His intimate relationship and fellowship with His Father
- His sense of God's timing
- His God-given authority
- His certainty of purpose
- His purity of motive
- His ultimate goal to finish the work
- His responsibility in stewardship

We are called to be imitators of Him, to follow in His
footsteps, to walk as He walked. We are now going to
consider some of the work that He did. He gave an account
to the Father of what that work was in John 17:

- *'I have glorified You on the earth'* (v. 4)
- *'I have finished the work which You have given Me to do'* (v. 4)
- *'I have manifested Your name'* (v. 6)
- *'I have given to them the words which You have given Me'*
(v. 8)

- *'I pray for them'* (v. 9)
- *'I kept them in Your name'* (v. 12)
- *'I have given them Your word'* (v. 14)
- *'I have sent them into the world'* (v. 18)
- *'For their sakes I sanctify Myself'* (v. 19)
- *'The glory which You gave Me I have given them'* (v. 22)
- *'I have declared to them Your name'* (v. 26)

We have already considered the wonderful ways in which Jesus glorified God and finished the work. Let us now look at the other things He did.

'I Have Manifested Your Name'

For the Jews, to call someone by name was not merely to give him his title but to describe his personality or character. This is what Jesus did. He revealed the personality, the character, the very heart of God, so that He could say, *'He who has seen Me has seen the Father'* (John 14:9). In the past God had revealed Himself in different ways and spoken through different people:

> *'God, who at various times and in different ways spoke in time past by the prophets, has in these last days spoken to us by His Son . . . '*   (Hebrews 1:1–2)

Oh, the wonder of the incarnation. Emmanuel, God with us. God revealed in the flesh. Everything He did showed exactly what God was like. The world's reaction to Him was their reaction to God. He brought reality to God's name. In the Old Testament God's name had revealed what He is like:

- *Jehovah-Sabaoth* – God of hosts (1 Samuel 17:45)
- *Jehovah-Elyon* – Most High God (Psalm 7:17)
- *Jehovah-Roi* – God my shepherd (Psalm 23:1)
- *Jehovah-Jireh* – God the provider (Genesis 22:14)
- *Jehovah-Nissi* – God my banner (Exodus 17:15)

- *Jehovah-Rapha* – God who heals (Exodus 15:26)
- *Jehovah-Shalom* – God our peace (Judges 6:24)
- *Jehovah-Shammah* – God is there (Ezekiel 48:35)
- *Jehovah-Tsidkenui* – God our righteousness (Jeremiah 23:6)
- *Jehovah-M'Kaddesh* – God who sanctifies (Exodus 31:13)

Jesus showed God by the way He lived. He revealed:

- the love of God
- the holiness of God
- the justice of God
- the power of God
- the feelings of God
- the faithfulness of God
- the wisdom of God
- the grace of God
- the joy of God
- the glory of God

He was the 'image' of God (Colossians 1:15). This is the standard He set for all Christians, that our lives might show what God is like, what Jesus is like. How true His words were: *'I have manifested Your name'*.

'I Have Given to Them the Words which You Have Given Me' (John 17:8)

The word Jesus uses for 'word' here is *rhema*. He always had the right word for every situation and always gave the word at the right time. They were not merely His words, but the words the Father gave Him to speak. How gloriously dependent He was on God for everything. Dealing with people with a variety of needs and in varying circumstances, problems or crises, we all realise how much we need the right word – not just our good advice, but a word from the Lord. When God called Jeremiah to the prophetic ministry he was so conscious of his youth and inexperience, but God comforted him with these words:

> ' *"Do not say, 'I am a youth,'*
> *For you shall go to all to whom I send you,*
> *And whatever I command you, you shall speak . . . "*
> *Then the Lord put forth His hand and touched my mouth,*
>   *and the Lord said to me,*
> *"Behold, I have put My words in your mouth." '*
>
> (Jeremiah 1:7, 9)

Jesus forewarned His disciples of coming persecution, arrest, imprisonment and trial, and instructed them:

> ' . . . *settle it in your hearts not to meditate beforehand on what you will answer; for I will give you a mouth and wisdom which your adversaries will not be able to contradict or resist.'* (Luke 21:14–15)

As we walk with Him, seeking to do His will, He will always give us the *rhema* word, the right word.

'I Kept Them in Your Name' (John 17:12)

As the caring leader, Jesus did all He could to protect His followers. He was always the Good Shepherd. He protected them by praying for them, by teaching them, by warning them, by leading them by His example, and above all by loving them. His love was long-suffering, kind and patient. He never behaved rudely, nor did He ever lose His temper. His disciples and the people marvelled at *'the gracious words which proceeded out of His mouth'* (Luke 4:22).

The truth Jesus gave them contained both teaching and warning. Both are essential for protection. If you only teach, you can be fattening your flock up for the kill. If you only warn them, they might die of malnutrition. Jesus' talks would include phrases like, 'Beware lest . . . ', 'Take heed . . . ', 'Don't be deceived . . . ', 'Beware of men . . . '. He warned them about false prophets and false teachers. When Paul shared with the elders of the church in Ephesus, he said,

> *'Therefore watch, and remember that for three years I did not cease to warn everyone night and day with tears. And now, brethren, I commend you to God and to the word of His grace, which is able to build you up and give you an inheritance among all those who are sanctified.'*
>
> (Acts 20:31–2)

How wonderfully Jesus kept His disciples. He could say to the Father after three-and-a-half years of His leadership that *'none of them is lost except the son of perdition, that the Scripture might be fulfilled'* (John 17:12).

'I Have Given Them Your Word' (John 17:14)

The word here is *logos*. This is the revealed will of God in doctrines, teachings and revelations as we find it in the Scriptures. Paul could say to the elders in Ephesus, *'I have not shunned to declare to you the whole counsel of God'* (Acts 20:27). We have already seen that real strength comes through the knowledge of God, so how vital it is that leaders, like Jesus, give the people the word. What a need there is today for good foundations of scriptural doctrine. We need a renewal of love for God which is seen in our love for His word, His truth, His revelation. It is the main means of being spiritually equipped. As Paul encouraged Timothy:

> *'All Scripture is given by inspiration of God, and is profitable for doctrine, for reproof, for correction, for instruction in righteousness that the man of God may be complete,* **thoroughly equipped** *in every good work.'*
>
> (2 Timothy 3:16–17)

Make it your desire and prayer that you may be able to say to Him, *'I have given them Your word.'*

'I Have Sent Them into the World' (John 17:18)

The product of Jesus' leadership was that His followers were trained and equipped to face the circumstances of life and ministry. They had already experienced this. When Jesus had sent them out, sometimes two by two, He had given them the power to preach the word, heal the sick and cast out demons. Now on this occasion He had just promised them that when He went back to heaven He would send the Holy Spirit who would empower them to be His witnesses.

One of the duties of spiritual leaders is to teach, train and equip people to be sent out into the world – into the world of school, college, university, family, commerce and profession; the world of missions and missionaries; the world of community and the nations of the world.

'For Their Sakes I Sanctify Myself' (John 17:19)

The Lord Jesus fully realised the responsibility of His task. He was dedicated to it. He told the Father that He had sanctified Himself for the work. He had set Himself apart, consecrated Himself. What a challenge! How blessed are the people who have leaders who have set themselves apart, dedicated themselves. Leadership is not merely a job, a position, a profession. It is a divine commission, a holy calling, to which people have given their very life. Why not pause now and sanctify yourself for those you lead? Dedicate or rededicate yourself. That's what Jesus did.

'I Pray for Them' (John 17:9)

Think of being prayed for by the greatest prayer ever. Always praying in the will of God; praying with the expectation of an answer, the prayer of faith; praying with the right motive. Praise God, for *'those who come to God through Him ... He ever lives to make intercession for them'* (Hebrews 7:25). It is great when leaders can truthfully say, 'I pray for them', not general prayers, but particular ones, praying for each individual trusting the Holy Spirit to show what to pray. Samuel said,

'...far be it from me that I should sin against the Lord in ceasing to pray for you; but I will teach you the good and the right way.' (1 Samuel 12:23)

Application

Let us pray for God's help to be like Jesus to:

- reveal His name
- give His *rhema* words
- keep those committed in His name
- give them the *logos* word
- send them out equipped into the world
- sanctify myself for them
- pray for them.

Chapter 15

The Prayers of Jesus

'I pray for them.' (John 17:9)

How wonderful that we have a record of Jesus' prayers for His followers. As we saw in the previous chapter, the prayers of Jesus were always according to the will of God. They were never self-motivated; they were according to real needs and were prayed with faith. Just as the Lord gave us a pattern prayer, in what we call the 'Lord's Prayer', so in John 17 He has given leaders a pattern prayer. I encourage all leaders to make this part of their prayer list.

'Keep Through Your Name Those Whom You Have Given Me' (John 17:11)

Jesus prays for His followers' protection. He has already told the Father, *'I have kept them in Your name'*, and now He pleads that they may be kept continually. There are many dangers: there are 'wolves in sheep's clothing'; there are many temptations; there are false teachers and false prophets; there is the world, the flesh and the devil. He prays that they may be guarded, defended, kept. I wonder how many have suffered because leaders did not pray for their protection!

'That They May Have My Joy Fulfilled in Them'
(John 17:13)

The Lord Jesus was a joyful person and He desired His followers to be joyful too. His main joy and delight was to do God's will. He promised them that, if they would abide in Him and keep His commandments, His **joy** would remain in them, and their joy would be full (John 15:10–11). He assured them that no one could take this joy from them and He encouraged them to *'rejoice because your names are written in heaven'* (Luke 10:20). He Himself *'rejoiced in the Spirit and said, "I praise You, Father, Lord of heaven and earth, that You have hidden these things from the wise and prudent and revealed them to babes"'* (Luke 10:21). Real joy reveals the reality of the Kingdom of God within us.

> *'...for the kingdom of God is not food and drink but righteousness and peace and joy in the Holy Spirit.'*
>
> (Romans 14:17)

> *'...the fruit of the Spirit is ... joy...'*   (Galatians 5:22)

Let's be joyful ourselves and pray for our people that they will be joyful too. What a difference joy makes. It strengthens God's people: '... *the **joy** of the Lord is our strength'* (Nehemiah 8:10). When Nehemiah and the people completed the walls and gates of Jerusalem, they *'rejoiced, for God had made them rejoice with great joy'* (Nehemiah 12:43). It was not a work up but a work out. Do you want a joyful people? Then pray, *'that they may have My **joy** fulfilled in them.'*

'Keep Them from the Evil One' (John 17:15)

The Lord knew His followers had an enemy. He Himself had been the object of attack right from His birth. He had endured and had been victorious in His forty days in the wilderness, where He was tempted by the devil. He was continually opposed throughout His ministry. Now, only a few hours previously, Satan had entered Judas to betray Him. However, He had continual victory and within the next few hours He was going to die and rise again, defeating the powers of the enemy and death itself. He is *'the resurrection and the life'* (John 11:25). His presence living within His followers would always be greater than the power of the enemy. His disciples would also be tempted and opposed, but through His name they would have the ability to resist the devil and cause him to flee. Paul reminded the Colossians that Jesus has *'delivered us from the power of darkness and translated us into the kingdom of the Son of His love'* (Colossians 1:13).

So Jesus prays, *'...keep them from the evil one'*: protect them, guard them, defend them, watch over them and preserve them. How truly this prayer was answered! What opposition and persecution the apostles faced. Most of them were eventually martyred, but God kept them to the end, giving them an abundant entrance into the divine glory. Oh leader, don't forget to pray, 'Keep them in Your Name.'

'Sanctify Them by Your Truth' (John 17:17)

The Lord's desire, and therefore His prayer, was that His followers would be totally set apart for God. He had been their living example of this. We have already seen that He had said to the Father, *'for their sakes I sanctify Myself'*. The Amplified Bible puts this verse this way, *'Sanctify them, purify, consecrate, separate them for Yourself, make them holy by Your truth.'* He wanted them to be people of God, people of the Word of God. Sanctification includes separation **from** the world **to** God. They were to be *'holy men moved ... by the Holy Spirit'* (2 Peter 1:21). Sanctification has been defined as 'the work of God's free grace, whereby we are renewed in the whole man after the image of God, and are enabled more and more to die to sin and live unto righteousness.' Sanctification is Christlikeness. Jesus didn't use these words, but He could have said, 'Make them like Me.' John wrote,

> *'He who says he abides in Him ought himself also to walk just as He walked.'* (1 John 2:6)

Let us walk like Him and pray like Him.

'I Pray ... For Those Who Will Believe in Me Through Their Word' (John 17:20)

What a prayer! On the day of Pentecost when Peter preached and three thousand were converted, Jesus had already prayed for them. This prayer includes the preparation of hearts to receive the word so that the seed would fall on good ground. Let us include this prayer for those we lead, so that those to whom they witness will have their hearts prepared to receive the truth.

There are times when we have the privilege of speaking to people, and it is obvious that their hearts have already been prepared. Someone has been praying. I was once travelling by train in the USA from Seattle to Portland, Oregon. At lunchtime I went to the dining car for a snack and, although most of the seats were empty, the waiter put me at a table where another man was sitting. We got into conversation. He was a high-ranking officer in the United States Air Force. Before we reached our destination I had the privilege of introducing him to Jesus, whom he received as his Lord and Saviour. A few days later, in the morning, I went to the church in which I was ministering, to see the pastor. As I went into the building, there was a man in uniform walking around. He was an inspector from the fire department, checking on the fire prevention plans in the church. We got into conversation and he told me that his wife, who was not a Christian, had bought a Bible six months previously and had been reading it to him every morning! That morning as we spoke he called on the name of the Lord and was saved. Someone had been praying *'for those who will believe through their word.'* What an encouragement to keep praying this prayer.

'That They All May Be One' (John 17:21)

Jesus prayed for unity: such a unity that would convince the world that God sent Jesus. No wonder the enemy attacks this indisputable evidence, causing divisions, schisms and disunity in the Body of Christ. Is it possible that sometimes there is disunity because we have failed to pray for unity? Thank God there are increasing signs of unity, especially among leaders, resulting in whole cities being affected. No one can make us one. We are one if we are true Christians. It is important to remember the following truths.

Our unity is relational

'... truly our fellowship is with the Father and with His Son Jesus Christ.'   (1 John 1:3)

'Our Father who art in heaven, hallowed be Your name.'
                                                    (Matthew 6:9)

Our unity is based on the death and resurrection of Jesus Christ, with the assurance that:

'... as many as received Him, to them He gave the right to become children of God, even to those who believe in His Name.'   (John 1:12)

Our unity is positional

In the sight of God we are one.

- One body
- One Spirit
- One hope of our calling
- One Lord
- One faith
- One baptism
- One God and Father of all ... (see Ephesians 4:3–6)

We are together

- Joined together (Ephesians 4:16)
- Knit together (Colossians 2:2)
- Built together (Ephesians 2:21)
- Made alive together (Ephesians 2:5)

We are fellows

- Fellow citizens (Ephesians 2:19)
- Fellow heirs (Ephesians 3:6)
- Fellow labourers (Philippians 4:3)
- Fellow helpers (3 John 8)

There is nothing in the world that can be compared to Christian unity. There are clubs, associations, orders, brotherhoods, clans, federations and unions, but none of these can compare with the unity that there is in Jesus Christ. This unity was purchased at a great price, the blood of Jesus. It is a unity that is eternal. It is based on the Fatherhood of God, the Lordship of Jesus Christ, the ministry of the Holy Spirit and the authority of the Scriptures.

Dangers of limiting the scope of unity

We must be very careful not to limit the scope of unity by choosing:

- **selective unity**. We must not choose the Christians with whom we wish to have unity.
- **denominational unity**. We must not confine the boundaries of our unity within a denomination.
- **doctrinal unity**. We must not limit our fellowship to those who subscribe to our interpretation of truth with a variety of labels such as Calvinist, Armenian, charismatic or non-charismatic. Won't it be great to find out who was right when we get to heaven and not be able to say, 'I told you so'?
- **unity according to leadership**. Paul spoke of those who asserted, ' "I am of Paul," or "I am of Apollos," or "I am of Cephas," or "I am of Christ" ' (1 Corinthians 1:12). There have been many movements named after their leaders. Paul's attitude was very different. He wrote,

    *'To **all** who are in Rome, beloved of God, called to be saints . . . '* (Romans 1:7)

> *'. . . with **all** who in every place call on the Name of Jesus Christ our Lord, both theirs and ours.'*
>
> (1 Corinthians 1:2)

> *'There is neither Jew nor Greek, there is neither slave nor free, there is neither male nor female; for you are **all one in Christ Jesus**.'*   (Galatians 3:28)

Let us believe it, practise it, declare it, pray for it.

'That They May Behold My Glory' (John 17:24)

For three-and-a-half years the disciples had observed the perfect life of Jesus. They had seen Him when He had no place to lay His head. He had been acclaimed by some and mocked and ridiculed by others. Some had wanted to make Him king and others sought to destroy Him. In a few hours He would be betrayed, arrested, scourged, spat upon, crucified. The mob would scream, *'Crucify Him, crucify Him.'* All kinds of indignations would be inflicted on Him. His followers would forsake Him. Peter would deny Him. Now, as He prays to the Father, He looks to the future and says,

> *'Father, I desire that they also whom You gave Me may be with Me where I am, that they may behold My glory which You have given Me; for You loved Me before the foundation of the world.'*   (John 17:24)

The cross is in the foreground, but eternity is in the background. Jesus wanted them all to see the splendour of His glory, the radiance of His beauty, the awesomeness of His majesty. Peter, James and John had had a glimpse of His glory on the Mount of Transfiguration. John wrote, *'we beheld His glory, the glory as of the only begotten of the Father, full of grace and truth'* (John 1:14). John had another experience of Him in His glory which he describes in the Book of Revelation. Jesus expresses His desire not only that they may see His glory, but they also may be with Him. It is His desire for all of

His people. What a prospect! Paul, who suffered so much for the gospel, said,

> *'I consider that the sufferings of this present time are not worthy to be compared with the glory which shall be revealed in us.'* (Romans 8:18)

This should be the prayer and desire of every leader, that those they lead will be with Him and see His glory. This is the encouragement in difficult times. This is the light in the darkness. This is the comfort in sorrow. This is the hope in despondency. His glory will be revealed and we shall see it. Lift up your heads, lift up your hearts. You **will** see His glory. On the Damascus road, Saul of Tarsus had a glimpse, *'brighter than the noon day sun'* (Acts 26:13). John *'fell at His feet as one that was dead'* (Revelation 1:17). We will see the *'brightness of His glory'* (Hebrews 1:3). The best is yet to come.

Jesus, having prayed these prayers, went to the cross to make the answers possible. Hallelujah, what a Saviour!

Application

Pray these prayers for those you lead:

- Keep through Your Name those whom You have given me.
- Let them have Your joy fulfilled in them.
- Keep them from the evil one.
- Sanctify them by Your truth.
- I pray for those who will believe through their witness.
- Let them all be one, and instruments of unity.
- Keep them till that day when they behold Your glory.

Chapter 16

Christlike Leadership

'... to reveal His Son in me...' (Galatians 1:16)

Paul's great desire in his leadership role was to be as much like Jesus as possible. After his three 'silent years' of preparation in Arabia, about which we are given no details, he returned to Jerusalem where he was introduced to Peter by Barnabas and spent two weeks with him. One can imagine how much he would have wanted to know about Jesus from one who had lived with him for three and a half years. After this he travelled to Syria and Cilicia preaching the gospel. There is so much Christlikeness in Paul, so let us be encouraged as we learn from him.

He Was Certain of His Ministry

'Paul, an apostle (not from men nor through man, but through Jesus Christ and God the Father who raised Him from the dead).' (Galatians 1:1)

Like Jesus, he knew beyond any shadow of a doubt what his ministry was. He was an apostle. It is so important for all leaders to know positively the ministry to which God has called them. We see situations through the eyes of our ministries. Can you write your name and after that put down your ministry? Check the lists in Ephesians 4:11; 1 Corinthians 12:4–11; 1 Corinthians 12:28–30; Romans 12:6–8. Paul asserted that no man gave him his ministry: it came from Jesus Christ and God the Father, who raised Him from the dead. What a comfort to know that his ministry was linked with resurrection power! So is yours!

Paul Was Not a Loner

'... and all the brethren that are with me.' (Galatians 1:2)

He knew his need of others. None of us can be independent. We all need God and we need other people. Many leaders today are isolated, and that is dangerous. We need others, not only their fellowship and encouragement but sometimes their correction. In the various countries where I have lived, I have asked God to give me men of His choice with whom I can have friendship, openness, fellowship and those who love me enough to reveal any 'blind spots' I may have. *'Faithful are the wounds of a friend'* (Proverbs 27:6). To this day I have such friends, and to me they are a gracious gift from the Lord. I need the Lord so much and I need them. *'All the brethren that are with me.'* If you do not have such friends, ask the Lord for them. Even Jesus had His Peter, James and John.

Paul Was Not Sectarian

'To the churches of Galatia ... ' (Galatians 1:2)

As we saw in Chapter 15 our fellowship is not meant to be limited either by denomination or doctrine. Of course we must be loyal to our church and churches, but just as we have personal needs to fellowship with others, so we need to have the right attitude to all churches who love the Lord. Paul did not have the situation we have today of multiple denominations. May we have open hearts to **all** of God's people.

Paul Served God with the Right Motive

> '... *to whom be glory forever and forever. Amen.'*
> (Romans 11:36)

Just like Jesus Paul sought no glory for himself. He confessed: *'I have been crucified with Christ'* (Galatians 2:20). Just as Jesus sought no glory for Himself (*'I have glorified You on the earth'*), neither did the apostle. His great desire which he expressed to the church at Philippi was that *'Christ will be magnified in my body, whether by life or by death'* (Philippians 1:20).

Paul Was Not a People Pleaser

> *'For if I still pleased men, I would not be a servant of Christ.'*
> (Galatians 1:10)

Paul was not interested in the approval of people; he was interested in God's approval. He preached boldly about truth and denounced the preaching of any other gospel. He declared unapologetically, *'if we, or an angel from heaven, preach any other gospel to you than what we have preached to you, let him be accursed'* (Galatians 1:8). The gospel of Jesus Christ, which declares that human beings are sinners who can do nothing to earn their salvation by good works or moral conduct, but need to repent and believe that Jesus died for their sins and rose again from the dead, is offensive to many. Like Jesus, Paul preached truth even though on many occasions it did not please people.

Paul Never Forgot What He Had Been

> '... *I persecuted the church of God beyond measure and tried to destroy it.'*   (Galatians 1:13)

He did not dwell on his past life, but he never forgot what he was until that day when he had an encounter with the living

Christ on the Damascus road. It is good to remember what we were. Soon after I was converted at the age of twenty-seven, an old saint gave me this advice: 'Meditate on the cross for a few minutes every day. If you do, you will always be grateful and you will always be humble.' Remembering what we were will make us appreciative of the grace of God and will help us to be more patient with others. Sometimes we wonder why people do not immediately grasp the truth we teach, but we forget how long it took us to understand it and apply it.

Paul Realised His Calling Was Determined Before He Was Born

> *'It pleased God, who separated me from my mother's womb and called me through His grace ... '* (Galatians 1:15)

What a staggering thought! What a mystery! Every leader needs to be reminded about the fact that our calling was planned before we were born. There is no resigning or retiring. God said to Jeremiah,

> *'Before I formed you in the womb, I knew you.*
> *Before you were born I sanctified you;*
> *And I ordained you ... '* (Jeremiah 1:5)

Think of this wonder. It pleased God to separate **you**, and put you in the ministry. No wonder it is described as a *'high and holy calling'*. Amazing grace!

The Result of His Ministry

> *' ... they **glorified God** in me ... '* (Galatians 1:24)

Like Jesus Paul did everything to glorify God, with the result that what he did caused people to glorify God.

Application

- Reflect on the wonder of God's call on your life which was planned before you were born!
- Do you know what your ministry is? If not, ask the Lord to show you.
- Do you realise your dependence on others?
- Have you the *'all the churches'* attitude?
- Ask the Lord to save you from being a mere people pleaser.
- Pause and reflect on what you were before God saved you.
- Remember your calling is linked with resurrection power.
- Covet that the result of your ministry will be that people glorify God.

Chapter 17

Summary

The chapters in this book have been intentionally brief. It is not the amount of truth that we read which is of greatest importance, but the application of it to our lives. Three things are essential in teaching. First, we must learn truth, second we must personally apply it, and third we should teach it to someone else. The complaint of the writer to the Hebrews was that Christians who should have been teaching truth to others were still on a milk diet: they had failed to lay the necessary foundations in their lives, and were therefore unable to instruct others (Hebrews 5:12). Here is a brief summary to help us in our application.

The Silent Years

Whether we are in leadership, or being prepared for it, let us embrace all the possibilities of the **now**. May we be diligent and disciplined in our pursuit of God. God does not call lazy people to lead. If we are faithful in a little, He will commit more to us. Jesus taught us that what we do in secret will be rewarded openly.

Into the Arena

God chooses the right time to launch us into our ministries. But it does not always happen in the way we expect. God clearly called me to leave business when I was thirty-seven

years of age. I had been much involved in evangelism,
speaking at Youth for Christ rallies in South Africa and seeing
many coming to the Lord. He told me through the word that
I had to return to the land of my birth and so we came to
Britain with a very dear friend of mine, Denis Clark. I had no
dates in my diary. No one knew me. I had gone to South
Africa soon after being converted and before that great event
I had been in the war, finishing as a major in the British
army. Denis went to Sweden for some Youth for Christ
meetings, and I was left wondering what I was to do. I was
called of God and had come to where He had sent me. Now
what? Through my daily reading the Lord spoke to me again,
reiterating that I was to return to the land of my birth, which
was Scotland. I took a bus from London to Glasgow, booked
in at the YMCA, got down on my knees and told the Lord
something He knew! 'Here I am in my own country.'

As I waited He put the name of a village on my mind and I
sensed He wanted me to go there, which I did. I booked in
at a little bed and breakfast cottage, took my Bible and
climbed a high hill from which I could see the entire village.
Now what? As I was reading 1 John 2, verse 6 witnessed to my
heart: *'He who says he abides in Him ought himself to walk just
as He walked.'* This raised the obvious question, what would
Jesus do here? I knew the answer was that He would be
among the people. So day after day, week after week, I went
to every home to speak to people about Jesus. He impressed
on me that He had not brought me here to be a good speaker,
but a good listener. So I would get into homes and people
would begin to talk, and so many times as they shared, the
Lord gave me an entry into their lives, assuring them that the
answer to every problem was Jesus. A good number came to
know the Lord and went on with Him. Now I didn't expect
this when I entered my particular arena – no big meetings!

One of my first preaching engagements came through
meeting a precious band of Christians who worked in a
factory. They were all blind. I wheeled an old pram with
amplifying equipment up a hill to a space outside some
factories, and at lunchtime as people came and sat outside,
we preached the gospel. Now I hadn't planned that either!

You have to leave the opening of the doors to Him. That was forty-six years ago now, and since that time He has graciously led me to so many countries and to so many venues. I have preached to Africans under a tree as well as at St Paul's Cathedral in London! The choice is always His. How exciting (and sometimes how scary)! I have often said to the Lord, 'I trust you, forgive me for feeling nervous!' I also tell Him that all the successes have been His, and all the failures mine. How gloriously faithful He is!

Whether you are in the arena, or about to enter it, you can trust Him. *'The Lord will guide you continually'* (Isaiah 58:11). As you look to Him He will enable you to fulfil your calling. He not only knows our needs but gives us the wonderful promise, *'my God shall supply all your need according to His riches in glory by Christ Jesus'* (Philippians 4:19). How blessed we are.

Jesus the Perfect Example

He came to serve and to love, and to live what He taught. He set a perfect example in everything. He taught us to pray. By revealing His own heart in so many ways, He revealed the heart of God. Some of that revelation came from what He said as well as what He did. As we read John 17 we saw His love, His desires and His prayers for His disciples, and saw a demonstration in practice of how leaders should lead. How very important to keep getting to know Him better and better, so that we can imitate Him.

Requirements of a Leader

We have seen how Jesus fulfilled all the requirements of caring leadership by:

- **His intimate relationship with Father**
- **His knowledge of God's timing**
- **His God-given authority**
- **His clarity of purpose**

- **His purity of motive**
- **having the right goal**
- **being a good steward**

The Work of a Leader

The work Jesus did amongst those He led provides us with a wonderful summary of what our work should be:

- **He revealed God's Name**. He showed what God was like.
- **He gave them the words that God had given Him**.
- **He kept them in God's Name. He did all He could to protect them.**
- **He gave them God's word** – the teachings, doctrines, truth.
- **He sanctified Himself for them**. He dedicated Himself to lead them.
- **He sent them into the world** – trained and equipped.
- **He prayed for them.**

The Prayers of Jesus for Those He Led

- **Keep them through Your Name.**
- **Let them have My joy fulfilled in them.**
- **Keep them from the evil one.**
- **Sanctify them by Your truth.**
- **For those who would believe through their word.**
- **That they would be one** – for their unity.
- **That one day they would be with Him and see His glory.**

The Leadership of Paul

Paul was an example of a leader who loved the Lord Jesus, sought to be like Him and knew that the main purpose of His life was to *'reveal His Son in me'* (Galatians 1:16). We can all borrow that same desire and, like Paul, be a God pleaser and not a people pleaser. Like him we must never forget what we were before our encounter with the Lord Jesus and should desire that everything we do will be for the glory of God; including the ministry God has given us. *'I have glorified you on the earth.'*

Learn, **apply**, **teach**, and the Lord bless you richly and use you mightily for His glory.

> *'...when the Chief Shepherd appears, you will receive the crown of glory that does not fade away.'*   (1 Peter 5:4)

If you have enjoyed this book and would like to help us to send a copy of it and many other titles to needy pastors in the **Third World**, please write for further information or send your gift to:

**Sovereign World Trust
PO Box 777, Tonbridge
Kent TN11 0ZS
United Kingdom**

or to the **'Sovereign World'** distributor in your country.

Visit our website at **www.sovereign-world.org** for a full range of Sovereign World books.